Contents

Acknowledgements

It is important to acknowledge the help and patience of many students and teachers who have put up with our research team in their classrooms. By our agreement with them, they must remain anonymous, but that should not disguise the fact that we remember every one of them and are deeply grateful for the way they not only tolerated our prying eyes and our equipment, but willingly responded to our questions and let us see their work. I think it was more difficult for the teachers than it was for the students. Students are used to adults in their classroom and come to expect that as part of school life. Teachers, however, are not used to other adults in their classrooms, observing and recording everything that happens. Without their courage and tolerance, the research reported in this book would not have been possible. I hope that this book goes some way to thanking you for your help.

Behind a lot of the data collection and analysis there has been a research team. Because of the low budgets we have had to work on, they have usually had to work for the lowest possible wages. As a group, over the years, they have shown the most amazing dedication to the work which was often boring and repetitive. Over the last ten years Anthea Clibborn-Brown has managed the administrative details of the research, observed in classrooms, and helped with the transcribing of the recordings. Phillipa Bowron did a lot of the data analysis in the earlier studies. Lynne Ward and Kathie Renton did most of the transcribing of the later recordings. Two PhD students, Sue Collins and Ronnie O'Toole, worked as observers in the later studies and helped with much of the preliminary data analysis.

My greatest debt is to Adrienne Alton-Lee. I had been involved in research on teaching since the 1960s, but it was her PhD, undertaken in the late 1970s, that shifted my research from teacher focused to student focused. It was her idea to trace the experiences of individual students so that we could determine what and how they were learning. The first student-focused analysis of classroom experience and learning was her PhD thesis. In the 1980s we worked together to carry out further studies of individual student experiences and developed the techniques that allowed us to determine exactly what and how individual students learned. In the 1990s she moved to Victoria University and I continued the studies on my own. But the direction had been set by her PhD.

Completing our team, I acknowledge the dedicated work of Roger Corbett, the senior technician in the School of Education at the University of Canterbury. He was the one who built and continued to develop and maintain the miniature individual broadcast microphones that the students wore during our studies. He developed and set up the system of video-recording using miniature cameras equipped with zoom and wide-angle lenses. At the beginning and end of each study he spent hours setting up (or dismantling) the equipment, hanging from ceiling beams, balancing on the top of ladders, and sorting and threading banks of cables leading to and from the cameras and the audio-receiver and the audio- and video-recorders.

Graham Nuthall
2004

In 2001 when Graham and I both had residencies at the Rockefeller Foundation's Study and Conference Centre at Bellagio beside Lake Como, we shared a garden studio furnished with a bench, two computers, and two chairs. There Graham used the uninterrupted time to analyse more of the data from the Project on Learning and every now and then he would tell me what he was uncovering. The fruits of those idyllic days are included here.

Graham left us with a barebones book. Since his death, a team of people convinced of its value, have worked with me to fill the gaps and Bev Webber at NZCER Press has managed the publication with enthusiasm, without fuss.

Not being an educator, I relied on the judgement of Graham's longstanding colleagues, people who had been immersed in international classroom research over many decades, people whose challenges and support sustained his efforts. One of these, Greta Morine-Dershimer, esteemed academic, fellow editor, and friend, helped shepherd the book from the outset. She provided most of the references, attended to technical matters raised by reviewers, selected and set additional examples from the classroom studies in the text. Greta knew the book intimately and was the perfect person to write the Foreword.

Graham intended to write a summary chapter. My gratitude to Ian Wilkinson and Richard Anderson who bravely took this on, engaging in the unaccustomed task of getting inside the head of another educator, setting their own ideas aside. Graham greatly admired Richard's body of work and he and Greta had both spent time with the team at the University of Canterbury. They experienced Graham's methods and outcomes first-hand, while Ian knew Graham and his work from his time at the University of Auckland.

I often called on colleagues from the University of Canterbury and members of the board of The Graham Nuthall Classroom Research Trust for professional advice. Even the week before he died, Graham was working with urgent determination to complete this book. He shared his ideas and hopes with Alison Gilmore, the Chair of the Trust and she has stood alongside me as we tried to fulfil our undertaking to him. I thank also Elody Rathgen for putting the basic text in order and Baljit Kaur for her knowledge of his publications. Sue Collins and Ronnie O'Toole generously offered their PhD theses for additional excerpts from classroom talk from the studies done under Graham's leadership. I am grateful also to Michelle Clarke and a host of others who provided additional references and checks on content.

Friends gave me professional support and wise counsel especially Peter Woods with legal advice, Josie and Ivan Snook, Dame Ann Hercus, Bob Manthei, Helen Shaw, Denise Sheat, and my sister, writer Rachel McAlpine, who named the book. And backing our efforts to bring his last work to fruition, our dear extensive family.

This is the book Graham was always about to write but deferred till he had finished yet another long academic article, densely argued, packed with facts, and fully referenced. When he knew time was short, he said he had to write it as he saw it. He no longer had time for ifs and buts, no need to qualify his true beliefs, not even time for citations. If you the reader see gaps or want to question his assertions, so be it. All he would ask is that you read it and apply what makes sense to you as you seek to understand the hidden lives of learners.

Jill Nuthall
2007

Foreword

In 1991 I was privileged to observe a day of data collection during one of the series of classroom studies Graham Nuthall was then conducting in Christchurch, New Zealand with Adrienne Alton-Lee. I was tremendously impressed and intrigued by what I saw. This research approach, begun collaboratively with Alton-Lee, was continued by Graham in a further set of studies. In this work Graham was able to bring together areas of knowledge too often viewed in isolation. As Jere Brophy has noted:

> This work was unique in providing access not only to students' public contributions to lessons and discussions but also their side conversations with peers and even the observations they made to themselves (when they thought out loud). The transcripts and related artifacts developed in this work constitute a uniquely rich corpus of data, which Graham mined successfully using unique analysis strategies to produce unique findings. (Brophy, 2006, p. 529)

The understandings he developed grew from use of both qualitative and quantitative research methods, encompassed insights into both teaching and learning, and described classrooms in which cognitive learning occurred in a social and cultural context. The extensive reports Graham published (e.g., Nuthall, 1997, 1999) attest to the international attention his perspective on classroom learning garnered.

International acclaim, however, was not Graham's major goal. He wanted to help teachers facilitate and expand students' opportunities to learn. Toward that end, he spent much time and energy during his final illness in writing this book for teachers. Though the studies were conducted in New Zealand, teachers elsewhere will benefit from the information contained here.

The Hidden Lives of Learners provides explicit examples of the public and private talk of students, illustrating the processes by which students learn new concepts, and also develop misconceptions, while working on classroom tasks. There are surprising revelations about how self-generated experiences influence what individual students learn, the extent to which students learn from their peers, and the degree to which peer status influences students' opportunities to learn. Mini case studies of three minority (Māori, Pasifika) students point up the critical importance of both classroom and home culture in the learning experiences of students. A final chapter by Ian Wilkinson and Richard Anderson summarizes the important ideas about student learning revealed here, and notes implications for teaching.

Teachers who participated in Nuthall's studies learned valuable lessons:

> [T]he thing … I continue to look at is how many times you have to revisit the same concept before the children actually grasp it and understand it. (Rathgen, 2006, p. 586)

> It really cut me when I found out that there were things happening in the class between the children and I didn't know it was happening … they were talking in a voice I couldn't hear. (Rathgen, 2006, p. 585)

Teachers who care about students and learning will be fascinated by the student voices that speak on the pages of this book, and what those voices reveal about student learning in classroom settings. *The Hidden Lives of Learners* is a generous gift from Graham Nuthall to teachers everywhere.

Greta Morine-Dershimer

Emeritus Professor, University of Virginia
Former Editor, *Teaching and Teacher Education* (1998–2002)
gm4p@virginia.edu

Introduction

Over the last twenty years or so I have given numerous talks to teachers, to principals, school advisers, and other educational groups. There seems, however, to be nothing more ephemeral than a talk given to busy professionals. No matter how interesting and thought provoking the talk, the reality is that the talk is given to only a small group of people, and its contents get rapidly forgotten as the pressures of daily life re-exert their influence on those who heard it. So I responded positively to the suggestion to make the more successful of these talks more permanent and widely accessible by collecting them together in a book. This was the original idea for this book.

However, what works well as a talk, accompanied by overheads, casual asides, and constant hand gestures, does not necessarily work well when translated into print. Consequently, the process of turning these talks into print has involved a lot of revising and rethinking of the original ideas. Sometimes the original examples and analogies seemed, on reflection, to be inadequate or even potentially misleading. Sometimes I remember deviating from the notes, trying to adapt to the specific worries or concerns of the audience, but could no longer remember what I had actually said. The result is that the original talks provided the starting point for this book, but what it now contains are the results of further thinking and reflection on the research and ideas that formed the basis for the talks. I hope that it is now substantially better than the original talks.

There are three things that the reader should be warned about this book. The first is that it is not a book about how to teach. There are already lots of books that give teachers suggestions and models of how they should manage their classrooms and teach specific topics. Packets of resources and materials are available that teachers can use in their teaching of mathematics, science, and social studies. Generally speaking, teachers can always use new ideas about the different ways to motivate and stimulate student learning, preferably ideas that have already been found successful by their fellow teachers.

There is, however, a potential problem with ideas and models about how to teach. In most cases, there is a description of what to do and how to do it, but no description of why it might work. There is no explanation of the underlying learning principles on which the method or resources have been constructed. The result is that teachers are constantly being encouraged to try out new ideas or methods without understanding how they might be affecting student learning. It's like being told how to drive a car without being given any understanding of how the car and its engine work. This is fine until some kind of emergency occurs —the engine makes a strange noise, the car won't start, or the driving conditions become dangerous. As a driver you need to do something different, but what?

The same is true in the classroom. A technique or resource that seemed to work well in your colleague's class, doesn't work well in your class. You need to make some kind of adaptation, but what? Unless you have a good understanding of how the technique or resource is supposed to affect student learning, your adaptations can only be trial and error.

I have become deeply suspicious (for reasons I will explain later in this book) of research on different methods of teaching. The danger I fear is that teachers will be required to follow teaching recipes. Research will be used by educational authorities to tell teachers what they should be doing, regardless of the particular needs of their students or the circumstances in which they are teaching.

In my experience, teaching is about sensitivity and adaptation. It is about adjusting to the here-and-now circumstances of particular students. It is about making moment-by-moment decisions as a lesson or activity progresses. Things that interest some students do not interest others. Things that work one day may not work the next day. What can be done quickly with one group has to be taken very slowly with another group. What one student finds easy to understand may confuse another student. In order to navigate the complexity of the circumstances in which a teacher works, it is not possible just to follow a recipe. As a teacher, you make adaptations. You must. The important question is: what adaptations do you make? You can do it by a kind of blind trial and error, but it would be much better if you knew what kinds of adaptations were needed, and why.

For this, a teacher needs to understand how different students experience the classroom, and how their experiences shape the changes that are going on in their minds. It is this deep understanding of the learning process that will allow a teacher to know what will work with a particular group or class of students, and know how to constantly monitor the effects of any particular method of teaching or learning activity. A teacher needs to be able to anticipate how a new teaching technique will work in her or his class, and exactly what to look for to see if it is working or not.

It is for this reason that this book is not about how to teach. Its focus is on how students experience classroom learning activities and how they learn from that experience. In other words, it is primarily about the learning process as it occurs in ordinary classrooms. It is about understanding why some students learn and others do not learn from the same learning activities. It is about understanding how teachers actually influence student experiences and shape their learning opportunities. To be precise, it is about understanding learning.

This does not mean that I will not be making any suggestions about effective teaching. Understanding learning has a lot of implications for effective teaching. For example, it will become clear, as we look at the research, that students learn a lot from their peers. Their motivations and interests, their attention, and involvement may all be strongly affected by their ongoing relationships with their peers. This means, of course, that teachers need to understand how peer influences work and that they cannot be effective unless they take the peer relationships in their classrooms into account. There is no easy or foolproof solution to this problem, but many solutions have been suggested. I will look at these suggestions.

The second thing that the reader should be warned about is that this book is based on research on teaching and student learning. Almost everything that is claimed about teaching and learning in this book is either based on research that I have been involved in, or on the research of others that I know and/or trust. Not all research on teaching and learning in classrooms is good research that can be trusted. There is not a tradition of research on teaching and learning in which researchers build on each other's results, gradually accumulating a body of well-established, reliable knowledge and understanding of how classroom teaching works. A lot of the research is carried out by people who are completing research qualifications or are also heavily involved in other teaching and professional activities. Around the world there are very few educational research institutions in which researchers can work full-time on specific research problems. This means that, although there are many published reports of educational research, you need to be very selective in identifying those that have something trustworthy to say about classroom teaching and learning.

For this book, I have drawn heavily on research studies that I have been involved in. As I will explain later in the book, it has been hands-on experience. I have participated in all aspects of these research studies from the initial discussions with school principals and teachers through to the final details of analysis of the recordings and observations of individual student experiences and of my interviews with the students. This means that it is not just the results of these studies (as they get published in research journals) on which I have based the content of this book, but also on the experience of getting those results. Being there, in the classrooms, talking with the teachers and the students, watching closely what is going on, is, in many ways, the stuff of the research.

For those who think that there is an excessive reliance on my own research, I plead the excuse that there are very few others around the world who have carried out the same detailed, student-focused studies that we have carried out. Looking at teaching through the classroom experiences of individual students is largely unique in the world of educational research. Where others have taken the same perspective, I have quoted and used their research studies.

So how reliable or trustworthy is the research on which this book is based? I think the answer to that question is that we have tried to carry out the research in the best possible way. We have tried to make sure that each finding has come up at least three or more times before we considered it reliable. But ultimately it is the professional teacher who is the best judge. If the insights and understandings that have come out of this research prove to be useful—give you a genuine understanding of what is happening in your classrooms and provide you with a solid basis for creating and adapting more effective teaching activities—then the research is trustworthy. Because that is what it was carried out for.

The third thing that the reader needs to be warned about is that there is no emphasis in this book on ethnic or cultural differences in learning processes. There is no question that there are significant differences in the educational attainment of students with different ethnic and cultural backgrounds, and that this is a very serious concern, especially for a teacher working in a classroom in which the majority of the students come from different ethnic or cultural backgrounds from her or his own. But there is no evidence that these differences in attainment arise from differences in the way members of different ethnic or cultural groups actually learn. There is no evidence that, given the same experiences, Afro-American, Polynesian, Māori, Pacific Island, or Asian students do not learn in the same way. As the evidence discussed in this book will show, the differences in attainment arise from the experiences that these students have (see Chapter 6). For example, in Chapter 4—on the influences of peers on learning experiences—there is a discussion of racism in the classroom and the ways that students interact with those of different ethnic or cultural backgrounds. This is not an unusual position to take. Many studies that have been concerned with how Asian students do better than American students on international tests in mathematics and science are based on the premise that it is differences in teaching rather than differences in immutable genetic inheritance that create differences in attainment. Until we have better evidence, it is wise to locate the problem in teaching and the culture of teaching rather than in the nature of the student.

The content of the book

The first chapter in this book deals with many of our commonly held beliefs about teaching and learning in classrooms. It talks about whether live teachers are any better than computers, whether award-winning teachers are always better than other teachers, what we mean by effective teaching. The purpose of this chapter is to clear up some of the common misunderstandings about teaching and to introduce some of the issues that will be dealt with in more detail in the following chapters.

The next chapter is about assessing student learning. In this chapter I try to clear up some of the myths that surround the use of tests and look closely at how students actually go about answering test questions. This helps clarify what we mean by knowledge and skills when we talk about students changing what they know and believe and can do.

The third chapter takes us straight into the nature of student learning. I describe the research studies that provided us with an insight into the learning process and a basis on which to predict exactly what knowledge or skills individual students would acquire from their classroom experiences. It is about what goes on in the minds of students as they try to manage and make sense of their classroom activities.

The fourth chapter widens the perspective on classroom learning. It looks at the way students' learning experiences are shaped by their relationships with their peers and by the peer culture in the classroom. It looks at how much students learn from their peers rather than the teacher. This leads into a discussion of the role that ability plays, or does not play, in learning. Our studies have shown that we need to rethink the commonly held belief that high-ability students learn differently, or more quickly, or more efficiently than low-ability students.

The next chapter takes us further into the learning process. It is about the messiness of students' classroom experiences and how their minds try to make sense of the fragmentary and confused nature of much of the information they experience. I take as an example a detailed look at the way an individual student learns, or fails to learn, a single but difficult concept. The purpose of this example is to illustrate the way a student's working memory is involved in the learning process. It leads to suggestions about how to develop students' minds in ways that will enhance their learning.

Chapter 6 looks at the extent to which ethnicity can be seen to play a role in students' learning. I make the argument that the teaching and learning experiences of students have much more impact on their achievement than their ethnicity does.

Ian Wilkinson and Richard Anderson wrote Chapter 7 which summarises the significant ideas on learning that are explored in the previous six chapters. They suggest implications for teaching.

1

CHAPTER 1

What do we know about effective teaching?

To be an effective teacher involves a high level of commitment—commitment to children and young people, to their wellbeing and future lives; commitment to knowledge and the importance of being able to think independently and effectively in a democracy; commitment to a profession that is dedicated to improving society. This level of commitment requires a strong set of well-thought-out beliefs about learning and teaching and the ways schools can foster the wellbeing and development of their students.

This chapter is about some of the beliefs commonly held about teaching and learning in classrooms. Many research studies of teaching over the last few years have supported some of these beliefs and contradicted others. For example, most of us believe that if we sit in the back of a classroom and watch carefully, we can tell how effective the teacher is. We get a feel for it. It's a kind of atmosphere thing. It has something to do with the way the students react and the way the teacher reacts to them. Some of us see it in how much attention students give to their work. We call it "time on task". Others of us see it as the quality of the relationship between the teacher and the students. The teacher clearly likes the students, and the students appear to like and trust their teacher.

The tradition of evaluating teaching in this way is long established. Some researchers, as far back as the 1920s, tried to make this method of evaluating teachers more sophisticated by developing checklists of the things the observer (the school principal, administrator) should look for. But research shows that faith in being able to judge the quality of teaching by observing is largely misplaced. Finding out how effective a teacher is at promoting student learning has to be done by other means. So why do we continue to believe that we can tell good teaching when we see it? That is one of the questions I consider in this chapter. Another (and related one) is what do we really know about effective teaching and student learning?

In discussing these questions, I want to introduce you to some of the research I deal with in more detail in subsequent chapters. The discussion will be a kind of ground-clearing one. It will, I hope, make clear not only what I think research has to say about some of the issues surrounding our understanding of teaching and learning but also, without going into formal definitions, what I understand by teaching and learning. The questions that I want to look at in this chapter can be briefly summarised as follows.

First, how do teachers differ from computers, television, or good books? This is a good question to start with because it raises the issue of whether teaching is a distinctly human activity. Could teachers be replaced with electronic machines?

Second, why can't we tell a good teacher by observing in that teacher's classroom? This question goes to the heart of what teaching is all about. Is it something visible or is it something that goes on in the minds of the teacher and the students, and can't be seen?

Third, why are there no universally good or bad teachers? This question is about whether the effectiveness of a teacher depends on the class or the material taught or the context in which the teaching takes place.

Fourth, why will public measurement of student achievement never lead to improved teaching? There are many who believe that to make teachers more effective we need to display publicly the achievement of their students using grade scales or other yardsticks. So why are formal achievement tests of so little use to teachers?

Fifth, why can't teachers become more effective as a result of using the best methods of teaching? When considering this question, I will look at what a "method" of teaching is. Does it make sense to describe teaching as the use of different methods?

Finally, I will look at the effectiveness of teaching based on learning styles. The focus on student learning styles is one of the newer developments in education, and there are many books on how to understand and make use of student learning styles. This development sounds like an important new one in understanding student learning (like multiple intelligences and personality types), but is it?

These are all important questions to consider if we want to understand teaching and learning in classrooms. Let's look at each one in more detail.

How do teachers differ from computers, television, or good books?

There is much talk these days about using computers or other electronic devices as ways of teaching students more effectively. It is similar to the talk there used to be about the use of radio and television and, before that, to talk about the teaching effectiveness of good printed materials such as books. Universal schooling was introduced to teach reading so that everyone could have access to good books, the Bible, especially.

Why do I think that computers will not replace teachers in the foreseeable future? The central business of teaching is about creating changes in the minds of students—in what students know and believe and how they think. The ability to create change means that, in some way, teachers need to be constantly reading the minds of students. Are their minds focused? What are they understanding, or not understanding? What do they really think?

None of us can know what is going on in the minds of others. But we have to do the best job we can, by inferring what others are thinking. For example, when we talk, we use indirect signs to monitor how our listener understands what we are saying. We watch our listener's face for signs of attention or distraction, for signs of puzzlement or agreement. Teachers need to be even more sensitive as they try to monitor the signs visible in the faces and behaviours of a class full of individual students.

As far as I am aware, only experienced humans have this awareness. And there are good reasons to believe that this kind of sensitivity is critical to effective teaching. Kounin (1970) described it as "with-it-ness". You are probably aware that one of the greatest enemies of effective teaching is student misunderstanding. No matter how well you describe something, how well you illustrate and explain it, students invent some new way to misunderstand what you have said. A considerable body of research in science, mathematics, and social studies teaching has uncovered the enormous range of different ways students understand the most obvious ideas and principles. And many have argued that the real business of teaching is the business of changing the well-established but inaccurate beliefs that all students have.

So the question implied by this is the following: what should teachers be sensitive to? In an early study of teachers' thinking, Philip Jackson (1968) found that experienced teachers develop a high level of sensitivity to students' level of interest, their involvement, and their motivation. Experienced teachers can tell from the atmosphere in the classroom, from the look in the students' eyes, from their questions and answers, from the way they engage in activities, how much the students' minds are engaged.

Effective teachers can use these signs to tell how effective they are being. They use these signs to tell whether they need to change what they are doing, to speed up or slow down, to introduce more or less challenge. This approach is based on the commonsense and widely held theory that learning is the natural consequence of actively engaged minds: if students are highly involved in the activity, they are learning.

However, the research shows that students get very good at playing the reciprocal game. They are excellent at knowing what signs the teacher is looking for, and making sure the teacher sees those signs. I watched a boy who was staring at his book but not reading anything start to whisper aloud to himself as the teacher went past, as though he was struggling mightily with what he was reading. But he stopped whispering when the teacher had passed and began idly looking out the window. Our own research shows that students can be busiest and most involved with material they already know. In most of the classrooms we have studied, each student already knows about 40 to 50 percent of what the teacher is teaching.

The problem is that teachers can become very sensitive to what their students are doing and feeling, but their focus is, as it must be, on managing the behaviour and motivation of their students. Changing what students think and believe requires more than just involvement and motivation. Being sensitive to student learning requires something more. I will explore this further in later chapters. In the meantime, I think we can assert that computers cannot interact with students with anything like the sensitivity required of good teaching. Computers can, of course, deliver information, edit grammar and spelling, carry out calculations, make visible material at the extreme levels of molecules or galaxies in ways that would not otherwise be available to students. All of this provides the raw materials for teaching, but does not, in itself, constitute effective teaching.

Why can't we tell a good teacher by observing in the classroom?

I almost answered this question in the last part of my answer to the previous question. A busy, active classroom, in which all the students are enthusiastically engaged in projects or activities that require them to think and solve problems for themselves, looks like an effective classroom. Teachers who can create and manage such classrooms are rated as excellent teachers. Many of the quality assurance systems used to evaluate teachers are based on the belief that we can tell from looking whether the teaching is effective and the students are learning.

But research suggests there are serious problems with this approach. First, this tactic tends to be strongly influenced by current fashions in teaching. If we all believe that teachers should have their students working in small groups in their classrooms, we give high ratings to those teachers who are using group work. If we all believe that students should do most of the talking and the teacher should talk relatively little, we are impressed by the classrooms where this occurs. All this is part of the popular tendency to think that "methods" matter. However, as I point out later, "methods" are a dangerous idea when it comes to thinking about effective teaching.

Second, the teaching that produces most learning in students varies from day to day, from class to class, and from time to time in the same class. Individual students can learn quite different things from the same class activities. What is important is matching the kind of teaching to the specific needs and circumstances of particular students. How settled are the students? Should I go back over what we did in the previous session? How difficult will they find it? How far can I push them? Do they need something different for a change? Should I give them another example to work on? What did the previous teacher do to put them in this mood? And so on.

What we see a teacher doing with a specific class may be quite different from what we would see the same teacher doing with another class, or on another day. For all the insights that direct observation might provide, we should not base our evaluations of teaching on some universal model or set of models of good teaching. *We simply cannot tell by looking.*

I'm not saying here that anything goes in teaching. It's not difficult to identify really bad situations in the classroom and to know when the students are not learning anything. But what we see in the classroom is just the background of teaching—the context within which professionally competent teachers may be more or less effective.

Why are there no such things as universally good or bad teachers?

The belief that there are good teachers and there are bad teachers is widely held. Some of us believe that good teachers are born, not made. Good teachers have the kind of personality that students find attractive and respond to. Teaching seems to come naturally to them. The teachers at the other end of the scale are those who rapidly lose control of what is going on in their class. They seem unable to involve more than a few students. There is a feeling that they really do not want to be in teaching. They don't like the students, and they (the teachers) don't like what they're doing. It seems clear that the students in their classes will be learning little or nothing.

But obvious as this may seem, it is possible that the same teachers, working in different circumstances, with different students, might perform quite differently. The question we then need to ask is: is it the teacher's personality and way of teaching, or the particular class of students or the topic, or the school context that determines how effective a teacher is?

There has been a lot of research on the personalities of teachers. Widely used personality tests have been adapted for use with teachers, and special personality tests developed that focus on how teachers interact with children. However, despite numerous studies, there is no consistent evidence that teacher personality relates to teacher effectiveness with students. Whereas one study shows one aspect of a teacher's personality is important, another study presents quite different results. Intuitively, we know the teacher's personality is very important. The problem, however, lies in trying to define what we mean by personality.

Most attempts to pin personality down to something that can be clearly defined end up saying that personality relates to how a person interacts with, or responds to, other people, and sometimes to how a person reacts to situations created by other people. We use descriptions like kind, patient, open, friendly, aggressive, sensitive, caring, introverted. In the same way, our attempts to be precise about a teacher's personality end up with a description of how that teacher interacts with and responds to students.

And that takes us directly to the research that shows teachers are not equally effective with all students, with all subjects (topics), or with all aspects of teaching. Teaching is interactive. How teachers interact with their students depends on the particular mix of students in their class. It also depends on how the students have learned to interact with teachers, on whether the topic is an easy or difficult one, and so on. This is why research that tries to describe the behaviours or methods of the best teachers leads nowhere.

What has always seemed obvious is that one of the best ways to find out about effective teaching is to study what effective teachers do. There have been several studies of this kind during the last 50 years. One major such study was that carried out by the Paris-based Organisation for Economic Co-operation and Development (OECD). Each of 10 countries undertook to carry out a study of their own, and the OECD staff then collated the results to produce a general picture of effective teaching in schools in the developed world.

In the United States, for example, teachers in seven schools were selected for intensive study on the basis of high student attendance, rising test scores, and an "excellent reputation in the community" (OECD, 1994, p. 33). In New Zealand, a sample of five teachers was selected on the basis of recommendations from the faculty of a school of education. The faculty members were involved in the school practice of their student teachers and had experience of sitting in a wide variety of classrooms. In each of these countries, the researchers extensively interviewed the teachers and observed them in their classrooms for about 20 hours each.

Hopkins and Stern (1996) carried out a synthesis of the findings of each country's case studies and identified the six most important characteristics of excellent teachers across all the 10 countries. Briefly, these were:

1. a passionate commitment to doing the very best for their students
2. a love of children enacted in warm, caring relationships
3. pedagogical content knowledge (for example, knowing how to identify, present, and explain key concepts)
4. use of a variety of models of teaching and learning
5. a collaborative working style with other teachers to plan, observe, and discuss one another's work
6. a constant questioning of, reflecting on, and modifying of their own practice.

It is not difficult to tell from this list the beliefs that the researchers in the different countries held about teaching. But does the list describe what effective teachers do? Consider what was involved in these studies. First, there was the need to identify the "best" teachers. In the United States, the researchers used rising test scores alongside measures of attendance and reputation in the community. In the New Zealand study, the researchers based their definition on reputation. Having identified the "best" teachers, the researchers then had to decide how to describe the teachers' teaching. They could have asked the teachers to describe their own teaching, but teachers are not good at reporting accurately what they do (for example, Good & Brophy, 2002).They could have observed and recorded what the teachers were doing in their classrooms. But how could they know they were capturing the teachers' best practice? Perhaps the teachers were working with an almost unmanageable class with high levels of absenteeism. Or perhaps they were working with a class of beautifully behaved upper middle-class students all eager to learn.

What the researchers would observe in these two contexts would be quite different, and they would have no way of knowing which aspects of what they observed were important indicators of effectiveness. In short, unless the researchers knew what good teaching looked like before they started, they wouldn't know what to look for or how to interpret what they saw.

The result of these studies of "best" teachers is usually a picture of what the experts currently deem best. Whatever is fashionable at the time determines what researchers look for and what they see.

Why will public assessment of student learning never improve teaching?

Another focus of research on effective teaching centres on sophisticated ways of assessing student learning. The idea here is that if teachers know exactly what each student is learning, they have a better platform from which to reflect on their practice and from there to improve the quality of their teaching. As you all know, this view is a popular one with politicians, which helps explain the constant push to increase the amount of national and international testing in order to hold teachers to account and, through the natural competitiveness between teachers and schools, facilitate improvements in the quality of teaching.

Unfortunately, as almost all teachers know intuitively, there is something inherently wrong with the tests used to evaluate teachers and schools. And, with some exceptions, they are no help at all in improving the quality of teaching.

The first problem is that we have accepted the myth that we can describe learning with numbers. Beside each student's name, we record sets of numbers: Child A got 35 right, Child B got 27 right, Child C got 42 right. Sometimes the numbers are the number of questions answered correctly, sometimes they are percentiles, and sometimes they are grade scores. But what do these numbers mean for teaching or learning?

Contrast recording numbers with recording the information that Child A knows the names of the planets that rotate around the sun and understands their relative size, but finds it hard to understand the distances between them and why it is so difficult to send a person in a rocket to any of the outer planets. She enjoys reading about and looking at pictures of the planets and knows how to find and use the NASA website. Or consider the statement that Child B understands the relationships between the shapes of houses in different parts of the world, the resources that are available for building them, the climate, and the ways in which their inhabitants use them. When confronted with a picture of a kind of house he has never seen before, this youngster can make informed guesses about what part of the world the house comes from, the lifestyles of the people who live in it, and so on. These descriptions of a student's knowledge are the kind teachers can work with. They allow a teacher to identify weaknesses or misunderstandings in the student's knowledge, to determine what the student needs to learn next, and to evaluate the here-and-now effectiveness of his or her teaching.

If, however, we believe that learning consists of filling the mind of a child with small interchangeable particles of knowledge that are all of equal size and significance—like beans in a bag—then the numbers would make some sense. Child C's mind has more in it than Child A's mind and Child B's mind. But nobody really believes that learning is like that. This approach calls on a simple 19th-century model of learning that worked when the curriculum consisted almost entirely of learning to read and write words, and being able to recall arithmetical facts and rules. It made sense to talk about the number of words a child could spell correctly, or the number of arithmetical facts a child could recite. Unfortunately, a lot of assessment in education still rests on this outdated model.

Percentile scores and grade scores are a little better at telling something about a student's knowledge or ability. They are based on comparisons between students. For example, a percentile score of 45 tells us that the student has done better than about 45 percent of his or her age group, and worse than about 55 percent of his or her age group. But like other kinds of test scores, percentiles say nothing about what that student knows or can do.

The concern here is that numbers in a school's record books are very good at serving political and bureaucratic needs (Berliner & Biddle, 1995). Because the numbers can be added and averaged, they seemingly indicate which students are best and which schools are best. However, they don't tell us what these students are best at. They don't say what the students have learned or understand (Nichols & Berliner, 2005). You might ask, does this matter? I'll return to this question in Chapter 2.

There is much more to be said about the myths that surround assessment. Again, I take up these matters in more detail in the next chapter. It is enough to say here that most of the current forms of assessment do not serve the needs of teachers or students and have little relevance to effective teaching.

Why can't teachers become more effective by using the best methods of teaching?

Within elementary and middle-school classrooms, teachers and students engage in a set of cultural routines during the school day. There are situations where the teacher talks with the whole class or groups, with the students sitting in their seats or on a mat on the floor. There are small-group activities in which the students follow instructions, do research, compare and discuss the results, prepare group reports or artefacts. There are individual activities—sometimes carried out as homework—in which the students complete written exercises, engage in a writing task, illustrate their work, engage in an art project. The nature of these different kinds of activities varies with the kinds of resources available (for example, computers, reference books).

Each of these kinds of activities has an accepted form. For example, the teacher-led whole-class (or group) discussion involves a complex pattern of teacher–student exchange that has remained largely unchanged since we began recordings in classrooms. The following is an example of a typical class discussion. Here, the class is discussing a quotation from a poem: "With fingers weary and worn, with eyelids heavy and red, a woman sits in unwomanly rags, plying her needle and thread."

Teacher:	I wonder if anyone can tell me what time in history that is likely to be? Suzy?
Suzy:	About the French Revolution. They're poor people.
Teacher:	Very good answer. I wonder if you could give me a further reason. Peter?
Peter:	Round about the Middle Ages?
Teacher:	It could be. Len?
Len:	I thought it might be about the time of the Bayeux Tapestry. Doing tapestry and that.

Teacher: Yes, it could. But I think we have had an answer so far which was much closer to the real time ...

Like all such discussions, this one is initiated by the teacher asking a question. A student responds and the teacher comments on the answer before asking a further question. Again, a student responds, and the teacher comments briefly, "It could be," before inviting a further student to respond. Finally, the teacher makes a more general comment about the students' answers intended to guide the discussion in a specific direction. At the core of this pattern of interaction is the question–answer–comment sequence. Typically, in classrooms, this pattern repeats over and over with variations (more student answers, different kinds of comments) and within the context of information provided by the teacher or other resources (in this case the quotation from a poem).

What is interesting about this example is that it is from a recording made in a Year 6 classroom in 1959. There is no reason to believe that it is not typical of this type of teaching in 1959. What is perhaps harder to believe is that such teaching is typical of teaching in present-day classrooms.

We talk a lot about teaching methods, especially in areas like reading. There have been bitter debates between those who advocate "whole-language" methods, where the emphasis is on using meaning and estimation, and those who advocate skills-based methods, with the emphasis on analytic skills and learning letter–sound correspondences (see, for example, Dahl & Freppon, 1995; Pressley, 1994; Stahl, McKenna, & Panucco, 1994). Every subject area has gone through periods where new methods of teaching were introduced and old methods disparaged.

The term "method" is a convenient shorthand for talking about teaching and about the things that teachers do. But it is dangerously misleading when people begin to think of teaching methods as the equivalent of medical treatments or agricultural fertilisers. It leads to the notion that we can compare teaching methods in the same way as we can compare the effects of different drugs or chemicals. It also leads to the recently popular demands that research on teaching should use randomised trials of the kind used in medical research.

In the realities of the classroom, methods do not exist. Every teacher adapts and modifies so-called methods. Research shows that teachers who believe they are using different methods may be doing essentially the same things, and teachers who believe they are using the same method may be doing quite different things.

Years ago, I was involved in a study with the late Nada Beardsley on teaching methods in reading. We observed in classrooms and got teachers to keep weekly diaries of the things they did with their children. I spent a lot of time with this data trying to identify patterns in the teaching so that, ignoring what methods the teachers believed they were using, I could discover the actual methods they were using.

No amount of analysis of the data threw up any patterns in the teachers' activities that would consistently distinguish different teachers. They were all using their own personal mix of activities and materials, adjusted to suit their understanding of what their students needed, both individually and as a group. The analysis was frustrating, and the study never published, but the work did make clear for me that method labels only approximately describe the realities of the classroom.

Of course, it will always be convenient to talk about methods of teaching in the same way as people talk about methods of parenting or methods of counselling. But a great deal of misunderstanding comes from assuming that activities given the same name are the same activities. Pharmaceutical drugs do not change their content when given to different people, but teaching methods do change when carried out by different teachers with different students. Unfortunately, researchers who conduct trials of new methods of teaching in, for example, mathematics or science, rarely examine how their methods are being used in the experimental classrooms, or in the "traditional" classrooms used for contrast. Consequently, they never really know what produces the results they get on their assessment tests.

The debates will continue of course. People will write more books about new teaching methods, and teachers reading these books will find useful ideas for adapting what they currently do in novel ways.

Why do learning styles have nothing to do with learning?

Recently, there has been considerable interest in learning styles. Not only teachers but also parents and businesses have started to talk about the need to consider learning styles. Boys are said to have different learning styles from girls. Ethnic minority students are said to have different learning styles from the majority students.

Assessment of learning styles is now a big industry, and there are many different ways of describing learning styles, as evident in Cassidy's (2004) review of 32 different tests of learning styles, each of which has its own theory and rationale. Perhaps the most common differentiation is that between those people who learn visually, those who learn verbally, and those who learn kinaesthetically. Then there is the distinction between those who learn best by seeing the whole before the parts and those who prefer to work from the parts first; or the distinction between people who learn best alone and in silence and those who learn best in a social context with background music.

Confusion around the concept of learning styles abounds. Some commentators claim we all have individual learning styles; others talk of us all falling into two or three different categories of learning styles. Some commentators believe that teachers should have different methods of teaching for each learning style; others think that students are best served if forced to learn through a variety of learning styles.

One thing is quite clear, however. There is, as yet, no valid research evidence to suggest adapting classroom teaching to students' learning styles makes any difference to their learning. So why has the idea of learning styles become so widely accepted? One reason is cultural. We live in a culture that emphasises individual freedoms—where choice increasingly is seen as a basic right. The idea that everyone is fundamentally different and has the right to be treated as different fits well with our modern culture. Schools should therefore become like supermarkets where customers can roam the aisles, picking and choosing whichever methods of teaching take their fancy.

I think an analogy with food is useful. We all have different food preferences, more so now than a generation ago when the variety of food available was much more limited. The fact that we all have different food preferences does not mean the metabolic processes by which we digest and use food are different. We might get our vitamin C from different foods, but all healthy grown-ups need 45 micrograms a day to stay healthy.

Similarly, students might have preferences for different kinds of classroom activities or topics, but the underlying learning process, by which their brains acquire new knowledge and skills, is essentially the same for all children. Getting all children to learn by sitting still in a formal classroom can be just as difficult as getting all children to have a sufficient intake of iron by eating broccoli.

In other words, learning styles are about motivation and management. They are not about learning. The distinction is an important one. The popular focus on learning styles illustrates one of the common confusions about teaching and learning. There is a strong tendency to equate motivation with learning. Much of what goes on in classrooms is based on the belief that if students are interested and involved in an activity, they will learn from it. Being attentive and engaged is equated with learning. However, students can be highly motivated and actively engaged in interesting classroom activities, yet not be learning anything new. Learning requires motivation, but motivation does not necessarily lead to learning.

How then can we tell when teaching is effective?

So far, in this chapter, I have not talked about what I mean by effective teaching. There are many different definitions of teaching effectiveness, and many different analogies used to describe it, but in my view, they all refer back to student learning, providing you think of learning in the broadest terms. Generally, effective teaching means students learn what you intend them to learn (or some part of what you intend). You may want them to acquire new knowledge and beliefs, new skills or different attitudes, or some mixture of all of these. But whatever you intend, in order to know if you have been effective, you must have some way of knowing what your students believed, knew, could do, or felt *before* you taught them and what your students believed, knew, could do, or felt *after* you taught them. Learning, of whatever kind, is about change, and unless you know what has changed in the minds, skills, and attitudes of your students, you cannot really know how effective you have been.

This is where it gets complicated. Our research has found that students already know, *on average*, about 50 percent of what a teacher intends his or her students to learn through a curriculum unit or topic. But that 50 percent is not evenly distributed. Different students will know different things, and *all* of them will know only about 15 percent of what the teacher wants them to know. So, at any one time, a teacher will probably be facing a class in which about 20 percent of the students already know what the teacher is trying to teach them, about 50 percent know something about what the teacher is trying to teach them, and about 20 percent have little or no idea about the topic. How can that teacher, and any other teacher, possibly teach all of his or her students effectively without boring the top group or completely losing the bottom group?

The criteria or signs of effective teaching

Let me lay out some of the elements of effective teaching, based on our research in elementary and middle-school classrooms and on the research of others, mostly in the United States. I would like to do this as a set of premises or underlying principles that we need to take into account when thinking about effective teaching.

First premise: students learn what they do. It took me a long time to understand this premise. If you go into a classroom and look across the room at what all the students are doing, what do you see? Maybe you see the students sitting at their desks or tables, copying notes from the chalkboard—notes the teacher expects them to learn by heart and reproduce in a test at the end of the unit. What they are learning here is what you see them doing: writing notes, coping with the boredom without complaining, and later memorising headings and details they only partially understand. Given the students forget most of the content of their notes after the rote memorisation and test, what they do in the classroom day after day is what they learn and become expert in.

If they try to make life more interesting by coercing someone else to lend them their notes, or if they try out new ways to tease and divert the attention of their neighbours, then this also is what they are learning. *We* tend to separate the management of classroom behaviour from the subject matter that we teach. But these are not separated in the students' minds.

This example is probably an exaggerated one, and not common in classrooms today, but it should serve to make the point. When we design learning activities, we need to remember that the activities students engage in when they encounter curriculum content become inextricably bound up in their minds with the content. We know intuitively that students associate the content with their interest and enjoyment, but we tend to forget the specific activities that are involved, such as writing about what they already know, waiting for equipment, competing for resources, asking their neighbours to tell them answers, diverting the teacher's attention, and so on.

Second premise: social relationships determine learning. It's very important to remember that much of what students do in the classroom is determined by their social relationships. This is especially so in high school, where students are more continuously and deeply involved in their relationships with their friends and enemies than they are in their engagements with their teachers. Even in the teacher's own territory, the classroom, the student's primary audience is his or her peers. The peer culture can create the belief that doing what the teacher wants is demeaning. When there is a clash between the peer culture and the teacher's management procedures, the peer culture wins every time. As I said before, more communication goes on within the peer culture than within the school and/or classroom culture.

Difficult and unusual as it may seem, long-term successful teaching involves working with the peer culture. Teachers therefore need to know who is in which friendship groups, who wants to be liked by whom, who has status, who is rejected. They also need to know the kinds of beliefs and culture—about music, clothes, curriculum, learning, co-operating, and the like—that hold students' relationships together. Since so much of what students learn about the curriculum they learn from and through one another, working with the peer culture is the only way we have of managing that substantial part of their learning. Some teachers have tried to deal with this problem by creating an alternative culture within their classrooms—a culture of mutual respect and co-operation, a culture in which everyone is expected to succeed in some significant aspect of classroom activities.

Third premise: effective activities are built around big questions. If we are careful about the design of effective learning activities, to the extent that our students are continuously engaged in focused learning behaviour, *and* we want to monitor what they are understanding and learning as they engage in these activities, *then* we have to spend much of our time and our resources on designing and carrying out the activities. Taking the time and the resources needed to design effective learning activities means covering a lot less of the curriculum. To justify this, we must make sure that the outcomes of these learning activities are really important, not only in the official curriculum but also in the lives and interests of the students.

Fourth premise: effective activities are managed by the students themselves. The ideal learning activity, in line with the previous three premises, has the following characteristics:

a. It focuses on the solution of a major question or problem that is significant in the discipline and in the lives and culture of the students.
b. It engages the students continuously in intellectual work of the kind appropriate in the discipline, which means that the larger question or problem must be broken down into smaller linked problems that are essential to solving the larger problem.
c. It provides teachers with opportunities, as the students engage in solving the smaller linked problems, to monitor individual students' evolving understandings of the content and procedures they must carry out.
d. It allows students, with experience, to manage their own learning. This is because a parallel goal of the effective learning activity is for the students to internalise the procedures so that they become part of their natural way of thinking.

Each of these four premises emerges again in the following chapters. There, they will be developed in more detail, and in relation to the research that lies behind them.

Acknowledging the extraordinary difficulties involved

It would be inappropriate for me to conclude this chapter without acknowledging the enormous difficulties involved in effective teaching. As I discuss later in the book, the education system, as we currently experience it, is not set up to encourage effective teaching. Being sensitive to the progress, interests, and culture of about 25 different individuals and creating new and genuinely worthwhile learning activities that engage the interest and culture of these different individuals, in a climate where boredom is the expected state and students are on their guard against being conned into being interested, are extraordinarily difficult tasks. They cannot be undertaken alone or without enthusiastic institutional support and rewards.

CHAPTER 2

Myths and misunderstandings about assessment

Assessment of achievement has become a big thing in education. Governments around the world take part in large-scale international achievement testing in order to evaluate their schools. National and state governments have introduced compulsory testing of student achievement, mandating the collection of test scores for evaluating districts, schools, and teachers. In many countries, especially the United States, state-wide testing has become a major factor in the lives of teachers and students. Politicians continue to talk about introducing new forms of national testing to evaluate and provoke schools into better performance. Parents, the media, and politicians have come to believe that making teachers accountable depends on the continuous administration of tests. But even though tests and examinations have been with us as long as public schools have existed, and even though branches of educational and psychological research focus on understanding and perfecting different types of testing and assessment, assessment is an area embedded in myth and misunderstanding.

Consider, for example, what we think about the qualifications students get when they graduate from high school. Graduation rates are often used to compare the quality of schools. At the same time, students take their graduation qualifications to prospective employers when looking for jobs, or they send them in with their applications for entry to colleges and universities. In this context, employers see the graduates' qualifications as indicators of achievement and ability, and often as indicators of capacity for hard work and commitment. What would happen if the graduate handed over his or her results and said, "Look, you should not take these seriously. I had very good teachers. I am really not as good as this." Or "I know these marks look very low. But it's not my fault. I went to a bad school with bad teachers. If I had gone to a better school …"

The fact is we cannot make up our minds what graduation qualifications mean. Sometimes we see them as the result of teaching (when evaluating schools), and sometimes as the result of student ability and hard work (in relation to applying for work). They can't be both, so what are they?

As far as I know, there has been no serious attempt in the public domain to sort out this paradox. Most people just accept both claims about graduation qualifications without noticing the contradiction. However, many teachers are deeply sceptical about what tests and examinations do, and they are, I think, more right to hold this attitude than they themselves believe. There is, in my view, much misleading nonsense perpetrated by experts in educational measurement who have not really thought through the implications of testing for teachers and teaching.

In this chapter, I want to focus on the use of tests and exams to assess student learning in ways that are useful for teachers. More specifically, I want to focus on forms of assessment teachers can use to evaluate student learning and, if they like, to evaluate their own teaching. However, in doing so, I need to clear up some misconceptions about testing in general, especially large-scale achievement testing.

Achievement tests assess motivation before they assess learning

Several years ago, I was involved in developing the mathematics tests that were to be used in the second international achievement study of mathematics and science (TIMSS 1999) carried out by the International Association for the Evaluation of Educational Achievement (IEA). One afternoon, we arranged with a local high school to try out one of the mathematics tests with several Year 10 classes.[1] I supervised the administration of the test, following the printed instructions for a test supervisor, explaining the test format, and encouraging the students to do as well as they could, especially on the more difficult items.

As I watched the students, and the afternoon got warmer and warmer, I became aware that very few of the students were actually focusing on the questions. Some were quietly reading the test, skipping from item to item, but not writing on the answer sheet. Others were doodling discretely on the answer sheet, and several had their heads down on their arms on the desk. It occurred to me that if I were one of them, I would probably be among the doodlers. I can never resist drawing little cartoons whenever the opportunity arises.

When we put all the answer sheets together from the different classes, scored the answers, and looked at the distribution of scores for the different parts of the test, we got the usual distributions. Some students got almost everything right; other students got very few questions right. There was no reason to believe, from the test scores, that the test was not a good measure of what the students knew. The standard statistical tests of reliability and validity (for example, correlation with other school grades) showed the test to be a good test of mathematical knowledge.

Later, in our own research studies, we looked more closely at how students answered tests. It seemed increasingly clear from our evidence that what students did on tests was primarily a question of motivation. There were those students who cared a great deal about trying to get all the answers right, and there were those who couldn't care less, no matter how much the teacher tried to motivate them. And then there were those who knew exactly what to do to get the right answers, and those who had little idea and who often just stared at the test.

I am now convinced that tests that have little or no personal significance for students and do not measure what the students know, or can do. Instead, tests reflect students' motivation and test-taking skills. This consideration applies to

---

1 New Zealand uses the term "Year" rather than "Grade" to differentiate annual levels of schooling. The first year of primary education is Year 1. Children start school at five years old. Secondary education covers Years 9 to 13, during which students are generally ages 13 to 17.

almost all the international tests of achievement and probably to many state- and classroom-based tests.

The tests and quizzes that schools and teachers use for their own purposes are more likely to produce valid results, but this depends on how these assessments are presented to the students. Taking a test is not a simple matter for any student. It requires a lot of dedication and skill to work to the limit of one's capacity. Routine quizzes and tests given to students who don't really care much about their school results will never measure students' knowledge or ability. Tests only become measures of student ability or achievement to the extent that the students are committed to the value of school and to the importance in their lives of getting good grades at school. Sometimes it is a case of liking the teacher and wanting to do well for the teacher out of loyalty and affection.

However, we still need to be cautious about the results of tests. The results may not reflect what students really know, or are capable of. When test results are reported, they should have attached to them an analysis of how motivated and committed the students were to doing well on the test. The only studies of the relationship between test results and motivation I have been able to find are studies of the way motivation affects the scores of job applicants on intelligence and other job selection tests. As you might expect, job applicants who are very anxious to get a job, and who believe that the company will take the test scores into account when making the selection, get better scores than those who are less motivated or do not believe that the company will take the scores seriously. I believe the same applies to students in school, although I am not aware of any study that examines the effects of motivation or beliefs about tests on test scores.

Why do we record test results as numbers?

If we look at the records of quiz and test results that teachers and schools keep, we see many numbers and/or letters (depending on the school's marking policy). What do these numbers and letters mean?

Obviously, they tell how many questions each student got correct on some test or exam. Higher numbers mean higher achievement. Some students get consistently higher numbers (or grades) and other students consistently get lower numbers (or grades), which confirms our belief that there are good or more able students and bad or less able students. But what do these numbers tell us about student learning? The answer is almost nothing. The students didn't learn the numbers or grades. They (hopefully) learned something else. But what? That is not recorded in the numbers.

So why do we create tests that produce numbers (or percentiles or grades based on numbers)? As I indicated in the previous chapter, the answer lies in an old and outdated belief about the nature of knowledge. This belief holds that knowledge can be broken down into little bits, like knowing how to spell individual words or knowing single arithmetical facts. It is then possible to count the number of words a child spells correctly, or the number of number facts the child reproduces. If all knowledge and ability can indeed be broken down in this way, it makes sense to have tests that allow us to count how much a student knows, provided we know which words and number facts are in the tests.

We still carry this belief around with us. A teacher makes up a quiz of 15 questions about the content of a science or social studies topic that she has just taught, or a test of six problems that require the students to use a newly taught mathematical procedure. The teacher scores the test and records the number of questions answered correctly. It is tempting to think that the student who gets the highest score on the test *knows more* than the student who gets the lowest score.

If two students get 15 out of 20 on a social studies test about life in Ancient Egypt, does it mean that they understand the role of women in Ancient Egypt society? Did the girls go to school? Were they taught the same things as boys? Could they divorce from their husbands? Could they become priests? What happened to them if their husbands died? What did a young woman do all day? And so on. It is not only a question of factual answers to these questions, but also an understanding of the general principles of social roles and the status that underlies them. And if one pupil knows all about the lives of girls, but nothing about women, she or he might get the same test score as another pupil who learned all about the lives of married women but had no time to look at the lives of girls. But since they got the same numerical score, it is assumed that they must know the same things.

But significant knowledge and ability aren't like this. It is not possible to break knowledge and ability up into little bits. Significant knowledge is about what we ourselves believe about the physical and social world and how we interact with it. Such knowledge, of course, contains bits of information, but at the deeper and lasting levels of understanding and meaning, it is seamless. However, before I illustrate exactly what all this means, let's look at how students answer test questions.

How students answer test questions

Let me try a little exercise with you. Below is a simple factual question of the kind frequently used in achievement tests. The question tests knowledge of the capital cities of the world. Laos is a landlocked country of about five million people that borders Cambodia and Vietnam.

- Which of the following is the capital city of Laos?
  - ✴ Laotse   ✴ Viangchan
  - ✴ Ban Nakang   ✴ Naphang

Unless you are an expert on world geography, you are unlikely to know the answer. Faced with this question in a test, you'd probably not get it right. However, consider another version of the same question:

- Which of the following is the capital city of Laos?
  - ✴ London   ✴ Viangchan
  - ✴ Tokyo   ✴ Paris

This time, I would be surprised if you did not get the answer correct. So, with reference to these two versions of the same question, do you or do you not know the name of the capital city of Laos?

The difference is not in the question, but in the alternatives you were asked to choose from. You can answer the second version of the question not because you know the name "Viangchan", but because you know about Tokyo, Paris, and London. What, then, is the second version of the question actually testing? Your general knowledge? Your test-taking skills? Your powers of deduction?

This example throws up the whole consideration of what test questions actually assess, and how we find out what they assess. This matter is clearly not a case of a student knowing the answer and therefore answering the question correctly, and of a student not knowing the answer and therefore answering the question incorrectly. We cannot assume that the number of questions answered correctly reflects what a student knows or can do.

Let's extend this example a little further. A test contains 10 questions about the capitals of South East Asian countries and the questions are all of the type of the second example. Students could get all the questions correct, *not* by knowing the correct answer to each question, but by eliminating all the obvious incorrect options. This would give the teacher a misleading understanding of what the students know or can do.

Traditionally, determining what a test or quiz question actually assesses (i.e., its validity) is the province of the test developer. Test developers have a range of statistical and analytical methods for understanding what a test question is assessing, and thus determining its validity.

Nobody thinks to ask the students themselves. Some years ago, as part of our studies of what students learn from their classroom experiences, we decided we needed a clearer picture of how a student's test score reflects his or her learning. We found that, despite thousands of studies of tests and of how to analyse their results, almost no one had done this kind of research. Two studies did ask children how they answered intelligence test questions (one was by the supervisor of my Master's thesis, Philip Lawrence), but not one dealt with achievement tests.

So we made use of data from our learning studies. For each study, we developed an achievement test that covered everything the teacher told us she or he intended the students to learn and hoped they would learn during (respectively) curriculum units in science, social studies, and integrated topics that also involved language and mathematics. After each study, we interviewed each student. We asked the students to explain, for each question in the test, why they had given their answers and what they were thinking at the time. In these interviews, we explored the students' understanding of each question and the knowledge they called on to answer it.

What we found was very interesting. Students' minds seem to have two systems operating simultaneously. One system is an intelligent memory search system.

It tries to refind, from whatever cues are available, the information needed to answer each question. The second system is a deduction or inference system. Its function is to work out, again from whatever cues or background knowledge are available, what the answer should be logically. This second system does not always produce an answer but it does indicate what could *not* be an answer, or what kind of answer is likely to be correct.

The two systems work in parallel, with the second system monitoring the results of the first. We found that the students in our studies rarely came up with an answer they had not checked for logical fit or consistency. The systems also work unconsciously. The students in our studies only became aware of them (and let us know about them) when they struck some kind of difficulty. For example, one student recalled two answers that were both logically compatible with the question, but became confused because he did not know how to choose between them.

The memory-search system

From our studies, we realised that, for students, searching the memory for answers usually involves using clues or associations triggered by the question. These clues relate to the meanings of the question, or to the context in which the students learn the answers. The following example from an interview with 10-year-old Jan shows it is possible for students to directly recall the detail of a classroom experience some considerable time later (in this case, up to a year later). The interviewer has just asked Jan how she remembered that mercury is the substance in a thermometer.

> *Interviewer*: Where did you learn that?
>
> *Jan*: Last year, Mr B said, 'Does anyone know what mercury is?' and Tony put up his hand and said ... Oh, no! ... Mr B said, 'What's in a thermometer?' and Tony put up his hand and said it was mercury. And it was right, and since then I have remembered.

Our recording of the original class discussion a year earlier showed Jan's recollection to be substantially correct.

> *Teacher*: (holding up thermometer in front of the class) And if you're very clever, inside it you can see ... there is a hollow part there that the silver stuff goes up in. What is the silver stuff called? Does anyone know?

Tony:	Mercury.
Teacher:	Is that right? It *is* called mercury. No question about that.

When the interviewer asks her, Jan also remembers her thoughts during that original experience.

Jan:	I thought, 'You [Tony] have got to be wrong.' I thought mercury was sort of a jewel or something like that. Or just a planet.
Interviewer:	So you thought he was wrong?
Jan:	Mm. I thought it was ink or water [in the thermometer].

Such recall appears to be simple and direct, although Jan also clearly remembers her doubts at the time.

In the next example, another student (Rata) tries to use recall of the relevant classroom experience to cue recall of the relevant content, but fails. The question she is commenting on asked her to recall the wind associated with very warm weather in Christchurch, New Zealand.

Rata:	Yeah, we did a chart on it, but I can't remember what we put on it now … this big picture on this big piece of paper on the wall. And our group had to do something on weather, and you had to write these, the north, south, east, and west on it, and see, and put, which weather brings the hottest (laugh).
Interviewer:	Right, and your group did that?
Rata:	Yes, and you had to put it up on the wall.
Interviewer:	Right, and do you remember which was the warm, dry one?
Rata:	No (laugh).
Interviewer:	Can you picture it in your mind, the one your group did? Who did the writing on the chart?
Rata:	Bruce.
Interviewer:	Did he? Did you help?
Rata:	Um, no, the other two didn't help us, only me and Bruce done it. I did some of the writing on it and he, he wrote it out, and I wrote 'weather', and he, um, we both thought it up, and looked on our chart [weather records] to see which one was warm.

The next example shows how students' long-term recall of prior classroom experiences contributes to their answers on pretests. In a science unit on Kitchen Chemistry in a Years 5 and 6 composite class, students are required to combine an acid and a carbonate to produce a chemical reaction that blows a cork off a bottle. In the unit pretest, one of the students, Jeff, recalls a kindergarten experience to explain how he knows vinegar is an acid.[2]

Interviewer: Way back on the pretest, did you know what an acid was then?

Jeff: Yeah, I know I put the vinegar and Coca Cola. I might have put lemon juice.

Interviewer: So you knew this before the unit, you think?

Jeff: I just knew what those two were. I wasn't sure about the lemon juice.

Interviewer: So where would you have learned way back about vinegar?

Jeff: Probably when I was in kindy ... 'cause you made volcanoes out of sand and then you (inaudible) ... just like in the unit, there has to be an acid and a carbonate.

Interviewer: Did you know that way back in kindy?

Jeff: Well, you didn't actually know if it was an acid or not, but you knew it had to have something, like, different to go with it.

The deduction and inference system

Usually, when recall fails, students try to deduce an answer from related knowledge. In the following example, Kim explains how he worked out that "fire" is the answer to the question, "What was the greatest fear of people living in medieval towns?" He remembered a picture he had seen during a unit on medieval England.

Kim: I can remember, um, in the picture, ah, I could imagine how fire spreading through there, spreading through it, 'cause the houses was very, very close together. Like, it's one big motel about as, um, big as a street. Yeah, not a fence or a garden, just the one big block of houses joined to the next one. No alleyways through.

Interviewer: Right, and can you remember Ms A saying that [about fire]?

Kim: No.

---

2 This interview, from Study 16 of Nuthall's Project on Learning, is quoted in Suzanne Collins' doctoral thesis (Collins, 2005, p. 303).

Interviewer: Well, how else might you have worked that out?
Kim: Ah, by that picture (laughs).

In the next example, the deduction is made from out-of-school experiences. Tui has paid little attention in class, but he makes frequent use of his home experiences to fill in for school knowledge. The question he is discussing concerns the weather conditions that precede rain. Tui explains why there have to be clouds in the sky.

Tui: Oh, 'cause me, and a few of the children, we went down to the shops to buy some fish and chips and all, the, there were all clouds. We thought it wasn't going to rain, eh, so we just walked off home, and it started raining. So we sat down under the verandahs [of the shops] and ate the chips, and when it stopped, we took off home.

Generally, it seems that the processes of direct recall and deduction work together. Memory search is itself a kind of deductive process, as cues (such as recall of class activity) are used as a focus for and evaluation of the search process. Sometimes, however, recall and deduction conflict with each other. When asked how she learned the name of the space between two high-pressure areas on a weather map, Rata recalls exactly what the teacher had said in class.

Rata: Yea, Mr B said, I think, it's a trough, because he said, he used, he put trough and ridge … on the [black]board for us. Something was low and something was high. He used one of those. He used 'trough' on it.
Interviewer: Yes, so you really think it was trough?
Rata: Yeah … But, I don't think it is that though.
Interviewer: Do you know what a trough would be, if it were what he was talking about, when he put it on the [black]board?
Rata: No, I thought it was something a horse drunk out of.

Rata rejects the name "trough" for a low-pressure area because she knows the word means "something a horse drunk out of" even though she clearly remembers the teacher writing "trough" on the blackboard.

In an interview following the Kitchen Chemistry unit mentioned earlier, Elle discusses her reasoning behind her answer to what made a cork pop out of a bottle.

Elle:	Probably because the mixture of vinegar and baking soda forms a bead as I said earlier on. They form a big bead and they form a sort of mix. They form a mixture and ... they mix together and form CO_2 and the CO_2 builds up the pressure and then slowly gets enough pressure to sort of push the cork out. So the cork goes flying. One of them, when we did that split in half ... it went zoom and then it went ... the bottle went flying about two centimetres up in the air.
Interviewer:	I like this idea of yours about a bead. Where did you get that idea from? Was it just something that came to you in your mind?
Elle:	Basically, yes. A big bead, with all these chemicals inside it.
Interviewer:	And then they push open?
Elle:	Basically. It's like a caterpillar. A cocoon. So the caterpillar ... there's a butterfly coming out of the cocoon, it's sort of like the CO_2 sort of nibbling its way out and sort of flying away.

Direct recall is rare

The above examples illustrate the complex processes that go on as students attempt to answer test questions. What should be clear from them is that there is rarely any such thing as direct recall. When students work to answer test questions correctly, they make considerable use of background knowledge and engage in intelligent search and deduction processes. No answer is trusted unless it makes logical sense within the context of the child's existing knowledge and beliefs.

Let me summarise at this point. When we ask students to explain how they go about answering test questions, we find the process they use is a complex and intelligent one, even in relation to simple factual questions. Knowledge is not tiny bits that we can count and represent by numbers, but a network of logically interconnected ideas, beliefs, and generalisations structured so it can be searched and used to work out and evaluate new ideas. When you worked out that Viangchan was the capital city of Laos (in the test question above), you used your network of knowledge about well-known cities around the world. Most so-called facts, if they are understood, are embedded within such a network of knowledge.

Forms of assessment appropriate for assessing student learning

At this point, I'd like to return to the original focus of this chapter—the use of tests and exams to assess student learning in ways that are useful for teachers; forms of assessment teachers can use to evaluate student learning and, if they like, to evaluate their own teaching. Let me begin with an idealised situation. Suppose you prepare a social studies topic on "Life in Ancient Egypt". You put together available resources (for example, picture books, websites, posters, maybe some artefacts) and plan a series of activities that involve the students in researching and writing reports on some significant issues: How long ago was the classical period of pharaohs and pyramid building? How did life in ancient Egypt differ from life in modern Egypt? What were the ancient Egyptians' beliefs about death and the afterlife? How were mummies made? How did children learn to read and write in ancient Egypt? What kinds of houses did ancient Egyptians live in?

You want to know how well the topic went. How successful were the activities in achieving your learning goals? For this, you need to know two things about each student. What did the student know and believe about each concept or idea *before* the unit began? What did each student know and believe about each concept or idea *after* the unit was finished? From this information, you can work out what each student learned and did not learn, or how the beliefs of each student changed during the unit. And by working backwards from the content of what was learned or not learned, you can work out what each activity contributed or failed to contribute to each student's knowledge and understanding.

The research experience described above strongly suggests you would find wide individual differences among the students. For some students, using the Internet to find out about housing in ancient Egypt would have worked well (their knowledge of the housing would be much richer and deeper than it was when they began). But for other students, using the Internet would have produced only superficial knowledge that has within it significant misunderstandings. If you can remember how these groups of students actually used the Internet, you would find clues (in the differences between the ways they used it) about why this activity worked for some students and not for others and what might need to be changed to make it work better for all of them.

Anything less than this is not a sufficient basis for evaluating your students' learning or your teaching. Anything less than this will not tell you that an activity worked very well because it was the activity that involved the students with some aspect of the content they learned. Or that another activity did not work because it did not engage the students with some part of the content they did not learn, or they misunderstood or were confused about. If you want to evaluate student learning and use that evaluation to improve your teaching, then you need to realise that nothing less than knowledge of how the students' beliefs and understandings have actually changed will serve these purposes.

Of course, the present circumstances under which you have to move through the curriculum means you probably won't have time to do this. So instead, you might decide to satisfy requirements by developing a quiz of 15 short-answer questions about some of the things you hope the students will have learned from their activities, and then recording for each student the number of questions he or she got correct. But what would you know about your teaching from that? If the students all got high marks, you could *assume* that the activities were successful, or that your test was too easy, or that it covered material the students already knew. Even if you assume that the test was not too easy and did not cover material most of the students already knew, you still have no idea which activities worked and why. Only when you know how a student's knowledge or beliefs have shifted, can you begin to identify the effect of specific activities.

I began this discussion by saying that what I am promoting here is an idealised situation. I realise it is difficult to fit this kind of individual interviewing of students into the busy day of the classroom. This consideration leaves you with two choices. You can reduce the time spent on assessment and make it useless, or you can reduce the time spent on the curriculum and use that time for effective assessment.

Examples of this kind of assessment are evident in various areas of the curriculum. Those of you who have used Marie Clay's Reading Recovery Programme will be familiar with the use of "running records" to assess reading ability (Clay, 1995, 2000). To produce a running record, the teacher needs to select for each student a passage of text that is at the upper margins of text that the student can read fluently. The teacher then sits with each student individually, listening to the student reading the selected text. As the student reads, the teacher notes, in his or her copy of the text, how the student copes with each word. If the student hesitates, how is the student working out what the word is? If the student makes a mistake, does the student notice it, and how does the student go about correcting it? What kinds of mistake does the student not notice? And so on. The result of this kind of assessment is that the teacher has an exact record of the reading skills the student has acquired, is still in the process of acquiring, or has not yet acquired. This knowledge allows the teacher to evaluate the programme the student has been following, and to develop a focused programme for the future.

Similar tests are being developed in beginning mathematics to assess how well each student is acquiring the different aspects of his or her understanding of numbers. Again, these tests must be administered individually, and again, they are based on a well-developed understanding of the stages that students go through as their concepts of number evolve. These tests allow teachers to evaluate exactly how effective their programmes are with each student, and to develop individually focused plans.

Work is also being done on developing ways to assess critical concepts in science and social studies. This work necessitates first identifying the central or fundamental concepts, principles, skills, and beliefs that students need to know and understand in order to progress in the discipline, and then undertaking extensive studies of students' evolving understandings and misunderstandings of these fundamentals. This second stage also involves identifying what a student needs to know in order to understand and learn one of these concepts. This information allows the development of methods of assessment that allow teachers to evaluate their programmes and to plan activities that will work best with their students. Again, this assessment needs to be conducted individual by individual, and embedded in a programme that fully considers individual differences.

Chances are you will have noticed that a move to individual assessment largely takes care of the problems of student motivation and engagement with tests. The concern about how motivation affects test results is a problem of mass and impersonal testing. That is why I have avoided talking in this chapter about what teachers should do, and instead focused on what an ideal solution to the assessment problem would look like. I consider the solution is whatever is logically necessary to serve the assessment needs of both student and teacher. I am well aware that achieving this ideal may be impossible in the current context of state-wide tests and relentless pressure on getting through the curriculum. However, in clarifying what assessment for effective teaching should be like, I hope I have indicated how teachers might work in their individual or political ways towards this ideal. I want to stress, though, that considerably more student- and teacher-focused research on assessment needs to be done before effective assessment techniques are widely available to teachers.

In the next chapter, I look closely at how students learn through their classroom activities. These considerations will then take us through to specific suggestions on ways to be an effective teacher.

3

Understanding how students learn and remember what they learn

In this chapter, I want to give as clear a picture as I can of the different ways students interact with, interpret, and learn from their classroom experiences. My intention is to let you see—as far as is possible—inside students' minds as they encounter all the different kinds of things that teachers require them to do.

The research studies on which this chapter is based differ from most of the research on teaching because they focus on the learning and experiences of individual children. Most other research on teaching takes the teacher's point of view, or the classroom perspective, seeing the students as a group rather than as individuals. But we have found that individual students can learn quite different things from the same classroom activities because they begin the activity with distinctively different background knowledge and experience the activity differently.

We therefore decided that if we wanted to understand how teachers shape student learning, we would have to begin with individual students and explore the varied ways in which they experience and learn from classroom activities. Over the years, through a succession of studies (for example, Alton-Lee, Nuthall, & Patrick, 1989; Nuthall & Alton-Lee, 1993), we have developed a kind of research technology that has allowed us to get closer and closer to the continuous experiences of individual students. I would like to sketch in this research technology so that you can understand just how we obtained our data and the basis on which we make claims about student learning.

How we carried out our research studies

Our first objective was to study student experience within the context of relatively standard or common classroom activities. When we first contacted a school, and the teachers in the school, we made it clear that we were there to study the ordinary experiences of students. We were not interested in the teachers or the quality of what they were doing. This meant quite a lot of preliminary talking, explaining what we hoped to do, and how we hoped to do it. In my view, the success of this kind of research depends absolutely on trust—trust between researchers and teachers, and between researchers and students. That requires a lot of talking about and transparency in what you are doing and intend to do.

During our early talks with the teachers, we asked about any topic in social studies, science, mathematics, or technology they each were planning for later in the year. Once we settled on a topic, we asked the teachers to plan their respective topics in the usual way, but to let us know as soon as possible what activities and resources they planned to use, and what they hoped their students would learn from the topic. We also asked each teacher about the students in the class and negotiated access to the records of the students' previous achievement and test results.

During these early stages, we communicated with the parents of the students in the class and with the school administrators about the nature of the project. We developed an illustrated booklet describing the purpose of the project, what we planned to do in the class, and what we would do with the audio- and video-recordings that we made in the class. We explained the procedures we would be using to ensure the anonymity of the school, teachers, and students involved. We also provided information about how parents and administrators could contact us so that we could answer any questions or concerns they might have. On sending the booklets to parents, we attached a letter that asked the parents to sign a consent form indicating they understood the nature of the project and the involvement of their child. If any of the parents expressed significant concerns or did not return the consent form, we did not work in that classroom.

From the information that each teacher provided about the content of his or her topic, we made up a test that covered, as far as possible, all that the teacher hoped the students would learn and anything else we thought they might learn from the resources they would be using. This process typically resulted in a test of 60 to 70 items, which we divided so we could administer the test in two sessions.

In our most recent studies, we confined our attention to four students in each class. We selected them by grouping the students in each class into boys and girls, and above- and below-average achievement (based on school records of standardised achievement and ability test results). We then randomly selected one student from within each of these four categories. Over several studies, we made sure that different ethnic groups were included in proportion to their numbers in the classes. Neither the teacher nor the students received information about who these selected individual students were until after the study was completed.

We then set up the classroom with our recording equipment. Miniature video-cameras with wide-angle lenses were attached to the ceiling in diagonally opposite corners of the room, so providing a view of the entire room. A further set of miniature cameras with zoom lenses was set up to focus on the selected students and those sitting around them. Each of these cameras was attached to the ceiling as far away from the selected student as possible so that no one could tell which person was the focus of the camera.

We set up this equipment several weeks before the unit began. At the same time, we introduced the students and the teacher to wearing miniature broadcast microphones. The students wore their microphones around their neck, where possible tucked inside their sweatshirt. The teacher wore his or hers on a convenient part of clothing. On the top of each miniature microphone was a switch that the student or teacher could use to switch the microphone on or off. The microphones worn by the four selected students were identical to the microphones worn by the other students, but they were the only student microphones that broadcast to a receiver attached to a bank of recorders located outside the classroom. During this preliminary period, we spent time in the classroom familiarising the teacher and students with our presence, getting to know their names, locations and working patterns, and explaining and demonstrating the equipment to them. For example, each morning before school, a number of the students watched and enjoyed seeing themselves on the monitoring screen that we set up in a corner of the classroom.

We administered the test on two separate days about a week before the unit began. We tried, by reading the test to the class and getting the students to focus on one item at a time, to overcome any difficulties the students might have. The test acted as our source of information about what the students knew before the unit began.

Once the unit began, we arrived before school each morning to test the equipment, synchronise our watches with the electronic timing equipment that sent time signals to the cameras and video-recorders, laid out the individual microphones on each student's desk, and prepared to start the video-recorders once the unit began.

In most of our studies, two or three of us sat in the corners of the classroom keeping a continuous written record of the behaviour of the selected students. We divided our observations into quarter-minute intervals, using a watch that was synchronised with the time-coding equipment on the video-recorders. Once the day's work on the topic was over, we photocopied everything each student had written or drawn, and made photographs of everything each student might have read or looked at.

Every morning, we asked the students to fill in a homework sheet. Here, they described any required or not-required out-of-school activities (such as writing part of a report, reading, talking to friends or siblings, seeking information on the Internet) that related in any way to the content of the topic.

About two weeks after completion of the unit, we readministered the test to the class to give us initial information about what they learned during the unit. During the subsequent week, we interviewed the selected students individually about their memories of the unit. It usually took a little time for the students to understand what we wanted, so during the beginning of the interviews, we invited them to say anything that came to mind as they answered the questions—any mental pictures, feelings, or thoughts.

> *Interviewer*: Now what I want you to do is, all the thinking that you do, think aloud, so that you can start talking as you're thinking—even if things are jumbled up or whatever—so that I can understand. (*Excerpt from interview with Tui*)

Because of the length and complexity of the interviews, we did not follow a fixed format. The questions typically asked for each item were:
- "How did you learn (know) that?" or "Where did you learn that?"
- "Do you remember that coming up in the unit?" or "Was there anything said or done about that in the unit?" or "Where would you have seen/heard about that?"
- "Did you know that before the unit?" or "Did you learn that during the unit?"

We used probing questions to find out more about any recollections the students reported.

The following excerpt from one of the long-term interviews (12 months later) illustrates the general nature of the questioning process we used. The focus of this excerpt was on the following multiple-choice item in the test: "New York city is made up of (a) three states, (b) four suburbs, (c) five countries, (d) five boroughs, (e) I don't know."

> *Ann*: I thought it was made up of five states … I know it's not made up of five countries. But it could be made up of three states.

> *Interviewer*: Right. Explain to me how you learned that.

> *Ann*: Um, well, I don't think it's five countries. I don't know why, but it couldn't be five countries, 'cause one country is America … And, oh, it could be five boroughs. But I don't think so … I don't know …

> *Interviewer*: Were you taught about it in class?

> *Ann*: Um, yes. I think we were actually. Well, that's all I could remember, five states. I think … I just, I don't know why, but I thought it was five states.

Interviewer: Right. And you've got a feeling it came up in class? Can you remember anything else? ... Can you remember the names of the states?

Ann: Yeah. I think it's actually three boroughs. It must be because it's not five countries, 'cause I remember that Manhattan was one of them. But I can't remember any other ones.

Interviewer: Was there a picture on the wall, or on the overhead, or in a book?

Ann: Yes. There was a picture on the overhead.

Interviewer: Can you describe that to me?

Ann: Um. Can't remember what it looked like. But I can remember that we had the overhead projector thing.

(You might have noted that this excerpt is also an interesting example of the interplay between searching memory and deduction described in the previous chapter.)

In the unit on Kitchen Chemistry mentioned in the last chapter, where an acid and a carbonate were combined to blow the cork off the top of a bottle, one test question asked, "What do you think happened to the baking soda?" This question was designed to check students' understanding of the difference between a solution like water and salt and a chemical combination like vinegar or lemon juice and baking soda. The salt could be retrieved from the solution by evaporation, but because of the irreversible nature of a chemical reaction, once the baking soda combined with the acid, it could not be returned to its original form. In an interview with Jack, the interviewer probed to check his understanding of this concept. Jack answered the question with one word—"fizzes".[3]

Interviewer: After it's stopped fizzing, is there any way we could get the baking soda back out of the lemon juice?

Jack: Probably not.

Interviewer: Why do you think that?

---

3 This interview from Study 16 of Nuthall's Project on Learning is reported in Suzanne Collins' doctoral thesis (Collins, 2005, p. 319). Sue participated in data collection and analysis for Studies 16 and 18 of the Project on Learning.

Jack:	Because how we were talking about salt before … salt is, it's different to lemon juice. Lemon juice is like a water, and salt's like a mixture.
Interviewer:	A mixture. So what would happen then with the baking soda and lemon juice when they combine and fizz? What is actually happening to these two things?
Jack:	They're getting weaker.
Interviewer:	They're getting weaker. Are they changing their form at all?
Jack:	Could be.
Interviewer:	What do you think happens to the baking soda?
Jack:	It would start to make it just go … bubble a bit more.
Interviewer:	And so how would that make it really hard to get it out of the lemon juice?
Jack:	'Cause when it's mixed, you never know how well it's mixed, and all that. So you've got to … you could try to get it out but [that] would be very hard … Could try to evaporate it out, but I don't think it would.

The next excerpt illustrates the difference in the interview procedures when it was clear the student did not know the answer to an item. The focus of the excerpt is an open-ended item that asked, "During the Middle Ages, 'charters' were important because they …?"

Sam:	I don't know.
Interviewer:	Right. That's fine. Was 'charters' ever mentioned at all?
Sam:	I think so.
Interviewer:	Just try and talk aloud about anything that you can remember.
Sam:	I can't remember about … I can't remember anything about 'charters'.
Interviewer:	That's OK. That's fine. Some of these things might not have even come up in class.

Each interview was carried out over three or four separate sessions and lasted for three or four hours in total. The purpose was to build a complete picture of each student's understanding of the content of the unit and their experiences relating to that content.

In some of our studies, we followed up the same students a year later and repeated the same interview to see how the passage of time had affected what they learned from the unit (see the interview with Ann, above).

Analysing the data

Dealing with the data was very time consuming. The first step was to transcribe the audio-recordings from the students' and each teacher's individually worn microphones. We then collated these transcriptions with the records made by the observers and with our photographic records of everything the students had written, drawn, read, and/or seen.

The next step was to go through these collated records of each student's experiences and, with the help of the video-recordings, identify which items in the test they related to. In this way, we built up what we called "item files" for each test item for each student. Each of these item files consisted of our recorded, photographed, and/or observed records of any experience the student had that related in any way to the content of a specific item. It contained, as it were, the life history of a student's experiences relevant to a specific test item. Since there were 60 to 70 items or more in each test, there were 60 to 70 separate item files for each individual student. These files often overlapped with one another, as experiences that were relevant to one item were also relevant, in a different way, to another item.

Finally, we categorised these item files according to the test and interview results. Those files in which the student knew the answer in the pretest and still knew the answer in the posttest were called "already known", and we set them aside for later use as a source of information about the student's background knowledge. We used the remaining files in our analysis of the student's learning. Here, the procedures that we developed, and that I describe below, for predicting what the students would learn or not learn were used to divide these items into those that were not learned—not known on the pretest and not known on the posttest—and those that were learned—not known on the pretest and known on the posttest.

When we did follow-up interviews a year later, we divided the learned items into those that the student learned but had forgotten a year later, and those that he or she learned and still remembered a year later.

Predicting student learning

In our very first studies, we had no way of knowing which items students would learn or not learn. In fact, we were, at the time, trying to find out what factors determined individual student learning. Discovering what was critical to student learning took a great deal of detailed analysis, but finally turned out to be something quite simple. If we think about a specific concept,[4] such as air pressure, the colour spectrum, ancient Egyptian beliefs about the afterlife, why people migrate, then we realise there is a certain amount of information that a student needs in order to understand that concept. This information might be, for example, a combination of a definition and a set of explicit examples. A student could experience this information in a variety of different ways, or in a variety of different parts or fragments.

We discovered that a student needed to encounter, on *at least three different occasions*, the complete set of the information she or he needed to understand a concept. If the information was incomplete, or not experienced on three different occasions, the student did not learn the concept. We made this discovery through the detailed examination of the experiences of three students in one of our earliest studies. Since then, we have applied this discovery to the experiences of many different students in different classrooms and used it to predict what they would and would not learn from their classroom experiences. We have found that, in each classroom, with each student and each concept that was not already known, we could predict what the students would learn—and what they would not learn—with an accuracy rate of 80 to 85 percent.

---

4 I use the term "concept" here as a general term for all the different kinds of things that the teachers wanted the students to learn and that we tested. Some of these things were general principles or ideas, some were facts, and some were procedures, understandings, and so on.

An example of student learning in a Year 7 class

What this kind of analysis involves might be better understood through reference to an actual example. The example I use here is a very simple one in the sense that the information the students encounter is much clearer and more coherent than is usually the case. The students featuring in this example, Joy, Teine, and Paul, are from a Year 7 class studying Antarctica as a combined science and social studies topic. One of the significant pieces of information their teacher hopes they and their classmates will learn about the climate in Antarctica is that it is the driest continent in the world.

On the second day of the unit, the teacher shows the class a video on Antarctica. As the camera pans across extensive scenes of ice and snow, the commentator says (among other things):

> … Another surprise is that it doesn't snow as much as you'd expect, except around the coast. Almost no snow falls on the high central plateau. In fact, less moisture falls here each year than in the Sahara Desert, making Antarctica overall the driest continent. The little that does fall can't melt, so it accumulates bit by bit. Over millions of years, it's compacted into a vast sheet of ice covering virtually the whole continent. …

A statement like this brings together in a student's mind a set of concepts that are (more or less) already known: snow, coast, high central plateau, moisture, Sahara Desert, driest, continent. A student tries to make sense of the statement by bringing these concepts together. Our observations and video-recordings show Joy and Paul apparently watching and listening to the video, Paul making occasional notes about temperatures, wind speed, and the ice cover, but not about rainfall, and Teine passing notes to her friends. But just before the video began, Teine and her neighbour, Leigh, had a whispered discussion about boyfriends. For example:

Leigh: (whispering) … Just try to be mature about this.
Teine: (also whispering behind her hand) Yeah, I know. But if she wants John—I mean she never acts as if she wants him. You know, like, I was …

During the video, the two girls continue this interaction by passing notes to each other. The following provides an example, in abbreviated summary form, of the observer's notes on Teine's behaviour over the first four minutes of the video:

Reads note from Abbie passed by Leigh. Scratches head and writes on note. Passes note to Abbie. Glances at video and looks at Abbie. Leans down to pick something up off floor … Receives note from Abbie. Watches video and puts note aside … Sighs, rubs eyes, and glances at video. Takes Abbie's note, rubs eyes, glances at video while fiddling with Abbie's note … Writes on the note and passes note to Abbie. Looks across at Leigh and Abbie. Watches video …

Immediately after the video, the teacher holds a whole-class discussion about the content of the video.

Teacher: OK. Put your hand up if you've learnt one thing from that [video] and you might like to share it with us. OK. Leigh?

Leigh: It's, um, it's a dry place.

Teacher: It's one of the driest places in the world. Why would it be a dry place, do you think? … That's something that surprised me, that it's a dry place. Good.

About 10 minutes later, in the same discussion, another student makes the same point.

Jane: It's even drier than the Sahara.

Teacher: OK. That the, that Antarctica is drier than the Sahara Desert. That might be a really interesting thing to find out. Why is it drier than the Sahara Desert? OK?

These statements repeat some of the information contained in the video commentary: that Antarctica is dry, that it is drier than the Sahara Desert. The teacher also repeats the claim in the video that this is surprising—and really interesting. Joy, Teine, and Paul appear to have been listening to the discussion.

The following day, the students work in groups, studying photographs of people working in Antarctica. Their task is to identify what the people in the photograph are doing, and why. The following discussion develops in the group that contains Joy and Paul (Teine is in another group). Their picture is of a person looking at some equipment on a tripod on the snow.

Maude: (talking of the person in the photograph) … Studying weather, yeah.

Paul: But this could be rainfall—rainfall for the week.

Koa: Huh?

Paul:	Could be rainfall for the week.
Koa:	Could be.
Maude:	How do you know rain falls?
Joy:	I didn't know rain falls in Antarctica.
Paul:	Rain does fall in Antarctica.
Maude:	Amazing!
Paul:	That's what turns this into ice.
Maude:	I thought, I thought, I thought it was dry.
Paul:	So it still has a bit of rain.

This discussion shows how a group of girls deal with a boy who asserts he is right when they believe he is wrong. It is clear that Joy has remembered what was said in the video, but Paul has retained his prior belief that ice implies rainfall. Teine's group, studying another photograph, makes no reference to the dryness or lack of rainfall.

Two days later, the teacher leads a whole-class discussion of the differences between living in Christchurch, New Zealand, and working in Antarctica.

Teacher:	What would you not see? ...
Nevin:	I was just going to say, you wouldn't see rain.
Teacher:	You wouldn't see rain. Why not?
Nevin:	'Cause it's the driest place in the world.

This time, this other student, Nevin, states there is no rain in Antarctica and explains it is because Antarctica is the driest continent. Joy, Teine, and Paul appear to be listening to Nevin's statements.

The next day, the teacher asks the students to write a report about what they have learned so far about Antarctica. Joy writes in her report that "It hardly ever rains in Antarctica ... Antarctica is the driest country." Neither Paul nor Teine refer in their reports to dryness or lack of rain. What the teacher wanted the students to learn was that "Antarctica is the driest of all the continents." But exactly what this means was left unspecified. Table 3.1 summarises the experiences of the three students in relation to this statement.

The table shows that Joy encountered the statement on three occasions (1, 2, and 4 in the table). She identified it as something she had learned in her report (5 in the table). She seems to have understood this to mean that it did not rain in

Table 3.1: Summary of the experiences of the three students in relation to learning of the idea that Antarctica is the driest of all the continents

Experiences of relevant content	Joy	Teine	Paul
1. *Video*: less moisture falls than in the Sahara ... the driest continent	Attending	Passing notes	Attending
2. *Class discussion*: one of the driest places in the world ... it's even drier than the Sahara	Attending	Attending	Attending
3. *Peer group*: (Joy) I didn't know rain falls. (Maude) I thought it was dry. (Paul) ... still has a bit of rain.	Involved in group discussion	In other group	Involved in group discussion
4. *Class discussion*: you wouldn't see rain ... it's the driest place in the world	Attending	Attending	Attending
5. *Writing a report*: (Joy) ... it hardly ever rains ... is the driest country	Writing report	Not in report	Not in report

Antarctica and confronted Paul with this fact in their group discussion (3 in the table). However, by the time she wrote her report, she had changed it to "It hardly ever rains." Joy's three direct encounters with the relevant information (1, 2, and 4 in the table) and her additional encounter when she wrote her report (5 above) ensured that Joy remembered this information. When we asked her 12 months later what she remembered about the climate in Antarctica, she said:

> It [rain] almost never falls. ... It's um ... it's too cold for it or something I think it is. It freezes up into snow or something.

When we asked Paul about rain, he replied:

Paul: Almost never falls. Because it, oh the rain almost never falls but there's snowstorms. Stuff like that.

Interviewer: Did you know that beforehand or did that come up during the unit?

Paul: No. It came up during the unit.

Interviewer: Think for a minute and see if you can remember in what way it came up.

Paul: Um, I think it was when they were telling us about it being the driest continent and that it hardly ever falls.

Interviewer: Yeah? And was that a person or a video or … ?

Paul: Um, video.

Paul had four relevant experiences (1, 2, 3, and 4 in Table 3.1). This was sufficient for him to recall the basic information ("the driest continent") 12 months later, but was not enough to ensure a clear understanding. He had forgotten that the voice on the video said it hardly ever snows. This was mentioned only once, and so was not remembered, leaving him with his prior belief that it snows a lot in Antarctica alongside his newly acquired belief that it is the driest continent.

Teine's experiences were different. She probably did not hear much of what the commentator on the video said. Her group did not discuss anything relevant to the climate in Antarctica (3 in Table 3.1), and she did not include any reference to climate in her report of what she had learned. Because of having less than three encounters with the relevant information, Teine, when asked in her interview about rainfall, did not remember anything about Antarctica being the driest continent, or about the lack of rainfall.

This example is a very simple one of an item file, because what the students learned was relatively clear (a simple, if surprising, fact) and most of their experiences were relatively transparent. For the students, the required information was obvious and easy to understand. Most item files are more complex than this. When the concepts are more complex and require difficult understandings, the relevant information can be fragmentary, only tangentially related, contradictory, or simply wrong. Students may develop significant misconceptions or confusions. Visual as well as verbal information may be necessary. But this example should illustrate the basic procedure for predicting what students will and will not learn.

In this particular study (on Antarctica), we predicted the learning of 468 concepts (an average of about 90 concepts not already known by each of the five students we recorded). Based on our analysis of each student's experiences, we predicted they would learn 301 concepts and not learn 280 concepts. We were right 80 percent of the time for concepts we predicted they would learn, and 82 percent of the time for concepts we predicted they would not learn. This is a much higher level of predictive power for student learning than has ever previously been shown in research on teaching. Our failures seemed to occur when students had significant misconceptions that we did not identify, when students worked out answers for themselves without relevant classroom experience, and when we probably missed (failed to record) significant experiences.

The success of these procedures also implies that other factors (such as the use of open-ended questions, feedback, advance organisers, relevant examples and analogies, and the interest level of the material) studied by other researchers may not be relevant to student learning except to the extent that they enhance the likelihood students will encounter more relevant content. But research on these teacher behaviours is so central to books on teaching effectiveness that we should keep an open mind on this.

How this learning occurs

It would be easy to conclude from the example above that learning depends on repetition. Repeat anything three times, and a student will remember it. However, students come to understand and remember many concepts without repetition of any single piece of information. Often they infer the relevant information from a related experience. In the following example, a Year 7 class is doing a science unit on light. The teacher expects the students to learn that the sun needs to be at less than 45° for a rainbow to appear. During a class discussion, some of the students think they see a rainbow out the classroom window.

Bettina: There, there. Oh you missed it [a rainbow] now.
Teacher: Can't see it because it's noon though. You won't get one, will you?
Bettina: Yeah, we saw one.
Teacher: No, apparently you can't get a rainbow at noon. No, you can't get a rainbow at noon apparently.
Derek: Can we go out and have a look?

The teacher does not say that the sun needs to be lower in the sky. She says that it is not possible to see a rainbow at noon. Here, the students need to infer that the angle of the sun is what matters. In the context of other relevant information, such an inference may not have been difficult, but the information the teacher presents is not the direct kind we saw in the Antarctica example, and the students are not learning by repetition.

In this next example, featuring another unit on Antarctica, the students are expected to learn how big the continent is. They work with maps of Antarctica, but none of the maps gives any indication of the relative size of the continent. However, a visiting speaker who has been to Antarctica gives them a clue, as she answers questions the students have prepared.

Paul: Have you been to the South Pole?

Visitor: No, I didn't go to the South Pole. And the reason for that is because Antarctica is so huge, it takes hours and hours to fly there, and they didn't want to waste petrol on us just flying there. Very few people actually get to go there.

The visitor's statement does not clearly say how big Antarctica is, but does suggest its vast size ("it takes hours and hours to fly" to the South Pole). The students know the South Pole is somewhere near the centre of Antarctica, and they possibly have some knowledge of how long it takes to fly between cities in New Zealand, and so they could construct from this knowledge some idea of the enormous size of Antarctica. Fortunately, for them, the same speaker provides, later in her talk, more definite information when she discusses how close Robert Falcon Scott came to reaching the South Pole.

Visitor: He got within 97 miles of the Pole. Now that sounds like quite a long way, but if you think about it, Antarctica. You know how big Australia is? You know how big America is? The United States? If you were to join Australia and the United States together, then you'd get Antarctica. I mean, it's that big.

This example should give a better idea of the patchwork of different types of information that students normally encounter as they learn new concepts and acquire new beliefs.

But all this still doesn't tell us how students learn. Why do they require at least three encounters with the complete set of information they need to understand a concept, no matter how fragmentary and indirect that set of information might be?

From the evidence we have accumulated through a series of studies, we have come to the conclusion that students must be using some kind of working memory in which they interpret the meaning of each new experience and in which they hold it until a new, related experience occurs.

Researchers investigating reading comprehension have reached the same conclusion. They suggest that mature readers are ones who have progressively built up a model of the meaning of a text by holding successive words and phrases in their working memory until able to make connections between them.

Figure 3.1 outlines how the working memory probably works. Classroom experiences are stored in the working memory as the student tries to make sense of them. This process involves making connections with prior knowledge and with other related experiences temporarily stored in the working memory. It also

Figure 3.1: How experience is processed and turned into new concepts in working memory

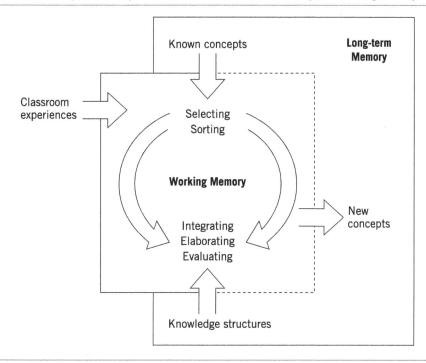

involves evaluating the new experience, and what that experience implies, against prior knowledge and beliefs. Finally, the new experience is integrated into prior knowledge, changing it, or being changed by it, depending on how it is evaluated.

For example, when Joy first hears during the video that Antarctica is the driest continent, she stores this information in her working memory and connects it to what she already knows about Antarctica and the Sahara. Then, during the later discussion, she adds Leigh's and the teacher's comments ("It's a dry place." "It's one of the driest places in the world") and Jane's claim ("It's even drier than the Sahara") to the information and its interpretation already stored in her working memory. The next day, when confronted with Paul's assertion that it rains in Antarctica, Joy draws on her working memory to argue that it does not rain in Antarctica. She also attaches the other students' comments to what is already stored in her working memory. Two days later, Nevin's and the teacher's comments ("You wouldn't see rain." "Cause it's the driest place in the world") are added to what is already stored in her working memory. By now, Joy has stored in her working memory several different versions of the information, allowing the working memory to make sense of this information and to integrate it into Joy's existing knowledge about Antarctica. When asked, the next day, to report on what she has learned about Antarctica, she reproduces the information ("Antarctica is the driest country") and adds, presumably because she still has some of the details of Paul's claims in her memory, "It hardly ever rains in Antarctica." Because of how this information has been integrated and elaborated in working memory, it has become part of Joy's long-term memory, and so she still remembers it a year later.

When a student encounters fragmentary information about a new concept, related fragments connect to one another in the student's working memory. Thus, the students in the Antarctica unit would have held the information about how long it takes to fly to the South Pole in their working memory until they encountered the statement about Antarctica being as big as Australia and America combined. One piece of information helped them to understand and consolidate the other. And when a student encounters new information that contradicts prior knowledge, their attempts to deal with the contradictions occur in working memory.

What our studies indicate is that new concepts are not created and transferred to long-term memory until enough information has accumulated in working memory to warrant the creation of a new concept. If this does not occur, the new experience is treated as just another version or aspect of a known concept and is absorbed into it, or is simply forgotten. It is as though existing knowledge and beliefs are protected against new experiences, unless the new experiences are similar and strong enough—have reached a critical mass—to warrant a major change or the introduction of a new concept or belief. Our data, to stress the point, suggest that three complete sets of relevant information, interpreted and integrated in working memory, are the minimum needed for the construction of a new belief or concept. In the normal course of events, this processing takes place unconsciously.

As an aside, I don't wish to imply that working memory is an actual place in the brain. Recent research indicates the whole of the brain is more or less constantly involved in processing experience, and so it seems more likely that working memory consists of those areas of the brain that are especially activated by incoming experiences. Its location, therefore, will be constantly shifting depending on where related past experiences are stored. It is tempting to suggest—although there is absolutely no evidence for it—that the construction of a new concept is the result of strengthening (and/or facilitating) new connections between relevant areas of the brain.

How do we know what goes on in working memory?

I said above that the processes that occur in working memory are almost always unconscious. As far as we can tell, Joy was not aware of what her working memory was doing with the information that Antarctica is the driest continent. How, then, do we know what goes on in working memory, and what is the point of trying to find out?

There are strong claims that how our minds process experience (that is, learn from experience) is not something we are born with, but something that is shaped by our experiences. The Russian psychologist, Vygotsky (1978), maintained that the processes we call thinking develop in the child because of the child's social experiences. The famous Swiss psychologist, Piaget (1928), made the same claim, except he posited that the child's interaction with the physical world is what forms the basis of the child's intellectual development. Even Freud made a similar claim when he proposed that the inner voice of our conscience is an internalised version of the voices of our parents, especially our father.

The general theory behind these claims is that we internalise what we do. As we build up experience of the world around us, we construct a model of that world that allows us to deal with it in our minds without having always to deal with it physically through trial and error. Our mental model allows us to anticipate and plan what we should do in order to solve problems, get what we want, and avoid dangers and mistakes. Working with our mental model of the social and physical world in our minds is what we call thinking. Much of this "working with our mental model" occurs through language, an internal version of language, or talking to oneself.

If this theory of how we learn to think and process experience is true, then examining what students do in classrooms should give us an idea of how school experience shapes students' thinking and learning processes. One of the things we found when we looked at transcripts of student talk, recorded on their individual microphones, was how easily and transparently the students shifted from social talk, to talking to themselves (or thinking aloud), to thinking inside their heads. Obviously, we could not hear what they were thinking inside their heads, but it was often not too difficult to infer, in general terms, what they were thinking from their writing, their chatter, and their relatively frequent episodes of thinking aloud.

The following extract (Figure 3.2) is from a Year 5 class doing a unit on the weather. As the teacher lists the names of the main types of clouds on the board, he asks a student to read each name aloud as he writes them. The individual microphones pick up the ways the other students make associations with the sounds of the words as they voice what they are thinking to themselves. This is not something that is required of them, or that is encouraged in any way; it seems to be a semiautomatic association process that we happened to catch on tape.

In the next example (Figure 3.3), the students slip easily between thinking aloud, talking to their neighbour, or just talking aloud. This is the same Year 7 class studying

Figure 3.2: Spontaneous talk during an episode on cloud types

Public discussion	Private talk to self
Teacher: This is the word. (writes "cumulus" on blackboard).	
Student: Cumulus.	
Teacher: Cumulus. (writes "nimbus" on the blackboard).	*Student*: (to self) Nebulite windows.
Student: Nimbus.	*Pam*: (to self) Numulus, nimbus ... Oh yeah, nimbus.
Teacher: (writes "cirrus" on the blackboard).	*Student 2*: (to self) Nebulus.
Student: Syros.	
Student: Cirrus.	*Rata*: (to self) Curious.

Antarctica encountered above. The teacher has been talking about the food chain and wants to develop a food chain that includes humans. Unfortunately, she starts with the wrong question. Remember as you read this that we could only record the talk of the selected students, so the private talk in this example is limited to the private talk of five students. Again, the private self-talk and the social talk provide insight into how the students are thinking as they react to the class discussion.

It is interesting to note how, near the beginning, Jim repeats aloud to his neighbour, Ben, what he has just whispered to himself. Joy talks mostly to herself, but once to her neighbour, Jane. Paul talks to himself and comments, to no one in particular, about Masako's response. It seems that when students talk to themselves, they do so not in some idiosyncratic private language, but in exactly the same social language they use with their peers. This is consistent with the idea that the language we use when we think is closely connected to the way we talk socially.

This detailed analysis of the self-talk and the private social talk of the students helped us confirm the kinds of processes most likely to go on in students' working memories. These processes are of the sort implied when we say students are "making sense" of experience, or "constructing" their own meaning.

Figure 3.3: Class discussion on the food chain

Public discussion	Private talk to self and others
Teacher: What eats us? *Paul*: Sharks.	*Joy*: (to Jane) I know, what we eat.
Jim: Lions, tigers, and bears.	

Teacher: OK. Carl, perhaps we should go
    backwards, then, and say what we eat
    then.
	Jim: (to self, laughing) Oh my. Lions and
	    tigers, and bears. Oh my!
	Jim: (to Ben, mimes eating) Lions and
	    tigers, and bears. Oh my!

Masako: We eat too much things. *Teacher*: Some of us might.	*Paul*: (to anyone) Correct Masako. Correct! *Joy*: (to self) What we eat.
Teacher: Right. OK. Jill? *Jill*: Fruit? *Teacher*: Fruit. (writes "fruit" on chart) *Student*: (inaudible) *Student*: (inaudible) *Teacher*: Was that fruit or food? *Student*: Fruit.	*Paul*: (to self) Meat. We eat apples, bananas, oranges, meat, mmm, fish.
Teacher: Fr-r-ruit. Joy? *Joy*: Fish.	*Jim*: (imitating teacher, to self) Fr-r-ruit. Ice cream.
Teacher: Fish. (writes "fish" on chart) Yes? *Sally*: Vegetables.	
Teacher: Vegetables. (writes "vegetables" on chart)	*Jim*: (to Ben) Vegebulls. *Ben*: Veggies.
Jim: Animanimals.	
Teacher: Yes Robin?	*Jim*: (repeating to self) Animanimals.

Robin: Pigs. Etc.	*Joy*: (to self) Animals. Meat.
	Paul: (to Robin) Vegetables, yellow
	    vegetables. We eat beef, yeah. (to
	    self) Meat.

As an example, let's look at a process that plays a critical role in students' engagement with class activities. We called this process "metacognitive monitoring". This is the set of judgements children make about how their own minds work and how they should think about a new experience. Students decide whether new information is difficult or easy, interesting or boring, familiar or unfamiliar, and respond accordingly. For example, in the class studying the weather, the teacher introduces the students to how to use a compass. He begins, as evident in Figure 3.4, by asking them what a compass is used for.

Figure 3.4: Class discussion of a compass

Public class discussion	Private talk to self and others
Teacher: What's it going to do for us, Lara? *Lara*: It tells us what is north, east, and south and west.	
Teacher: How does it do that, therefore, Noel? *Noel*: It's kind of like a magnet.	*Pam*: (whispering to peer) I know how it works. My father's got one. I mean my mum's father.

Pam decides for herself that she already knows how a compass works. Unfortunately, for her, her idea of how it works is different from the teacher's idea. The teacher wants the class to understand how a magnet always turns to point north/south. Pam thinks being able to use the compass in the way she uses it at home is all she needs to know. She consequently pays little attention to the teacher's demonstrations of how magnets work. Later, in the same class discussion about the compass, when the teacher starts discussing how the class will use this instrument, Tui makes it clear what he thinks about the compass.

Teacher: OK. What use is the compass going to be to us?
Tui: (to himself) Nothing.

Tui accordingly decides to get ahead by starting the cover page of his report while the teacher demonstrates how to use the compass. He starts drawing a large coloured heading ("About the Weather") and tries to engage the students sitting next to him in an alternative conversation in which he assumes the authority of knowing what is required.

> Tui: (whispering to those sitting next to him) I'm doing my project [on the weather] now ... How do you spell 'about the weather'? (continues writing and organising different coloured pens)

Because of missing the class discussion on the compass, Tui continues to believe that the wind determines the direction of a compass needle, and that wind direction is described by where the wind is going to and not where it is coming from.

In another instance related to the unit on the weather, the teacher asks the students to try to predict the next day's weather from a copy of the day's weather map. Only some of the students (including Rata) seem to be aware that the task is almost impossible.

> Rata: (looking at weather map) See. Anticyclone, high, it's coming onto New Zealand.
>
> Student: So there's an anticyclone.
>
> Rata: Oh, God, this is hard.
>
> Student: There's a big cold front coming.
>
> Rata: Oh, God, there is too. Look, there's a big cold front coming through Sydney. See, you can tell cold. See that shape of it.

Unlike many of the other students, Rata tries to focus on all the details in the weather map, and struggles to make sense of their implications. Her judgement about the difficulty of the task ("Oh, God, this is hard") is based on her understanding of the nature of the task and of her own abilities and knowledge in relation to it. Other students, who do not understand the nature of the task, focus on descriptions of the weather map without attempting to interpret it.

It seems likely that the way students understand tasks and how to carry them out depends on the kind of metacognitive judgements they make about the significance of the tasks and how these relate to their own abilities and knowledge. Tui, as the compass episode above indicates, often separated himself from class activities, judging them irrelevant or beneath his status as self-styled group leader. When we asked him how he had learned about rainbows, he attributed his learning to his mother.

Tui: … like the sun on the rain makes rainbow, it sort of mixes in, that's how all colours come out or something.

Interviewer: How did you learn that, Tui?

Tui: Well Mum used to talk about sun showers and about under the rainbow … what's that mean, and she would say sun on the rainbow.

Interviewer: Did it come up during class?

Tui: Yep.

Interviewer: Tell me about that.

Tui: Well some days when I am at school, it's not so hot or not so cold, just warm, and then we see this rainbow pop up.

Interviewer: And did people discuss it?

Tui: Well we just look at it and get on with our work.

When the interviewer asked Tui if "it" had ever come up in class, Tui had no recall of the teacher talking about it and interpreted the question to mean: did you see a rainbow in class? This was typical of Tui's responses. Because he frequently opted out of the class activities, or redesigned them to fit his own purposes, he had very little memory of the public class activities, their content, or purposes.

I will discuss the cognitive processes that go on in working memory in more depth in later chapters. As we will see, a student's working memory is an extraordinarily busy place. It probably handles large numbers of evolving concepts or ideas simultaneously. In most of our studies, the teachers intended the students to learn an average of 50 to 60 new concepts, principles, ideas. Given that the students individually knew nearly half of these before the unit began, their working memory would have been handling 25 to 30 new concepts by part-way through the unit. And given they would have been processing the same numbers of concepts in their social studies, mathematics, and reading activities, the total each student was handling simultaneously would have been nearly 100.

Implications for teaching

Three main points arise from this analysis of the learning process. The first is that student learning primarily depends on the information they are exposed to. This means that activities need careful designing so that students cannot avoid interacting with this relevant information. It also means being very careful about the form of the information that is encountered. There is considerable research (for example, Nuthall, 1999) to show the ways students understand and interact with information depend on their prior knowledge and understandings. Teachers often prepare materials and use analogies and examples that make new information clear and understandable, only to find students' prior knowledge and/or beliefs lead to new and unique misunderstandings. This situation can be very frustrating and unpredictable unless the teacher has considerable experience in teaching the particular topic or, in other words, "has seen it all before".

The implication of this consideration is the need for constant monitoring of students' understandings of key concepts and ideas. A few studies have attempted to help teachers focus their teaching on what their students know and do not know.

The head of science education at Stanford University (Professor Richard Shavelson) has been working with a group of science teachers to determine what they need to know to guide their teaching, and how best to provide them with that information (Shavelson, 2006). He has found it difficult to get teachers to think of test results as indicators of their own teaching, and not just as ways of evaluating students. Shavelson's work also shows that when given relevant information about their students' understandings and knowledge, teachers are not quite certain what to do with that information. Changing these types of thinking requires a new way of thinking that sees teaching as the problem, not the students.

A group in the United Kingdom (Leach & Scott, 2002) has been working with the idea that all teaching should rest on analysing what the students know before a unit and then comparing that knowledge with the knowledge embodied in the intended outcomes of the unit. They describe the difference between a detailed analysis of what the students already know and believe and the intended outcomes as the "learning demand". Through this process, teachers can match the content of the unit to exactly what the students need to know, and they can relate the activities in the unit to the students' prior knowledge.

While this is a start, there still needs to be constant monitoring of the development of new ideas and understandings as the unit progresses. This means building in activities, such as discussions or quizzes, designed to reveal how the students are thinking about key concepts or ideas.

The second main point is that students need time to process new concepts. As we have emphasised, our studies indicate they need to be taught the concept, or to encounter a full explanation of the concept, at least three times. As I explain in more detail in Chapter 5, this does not mean simple repetition. Simply repeating explanations or activities is likely to be boring and turn students off engaging with the content in appropriate ways. What it does seem to mean is that students' minds need time to process new information. They need opportunities to come at the material in different ways. It also means that the single brilliant explanation is not, in itself, enough.

We have all probably experienced attending a stimulating lecture, or reading a well-written technical book, only to find, when asked to talk about what the lecture or book was about, that the actual content has quickly faded from memory. We are left with the impression that the book was well written, or the lecture fascinating, and that we learned and understood many new ideas, but we have only the vaguest idea of what we actually read or heard. I once went to a superb lecture by the famous theoretical physicist, Gell Mann, on the latest developments in particle physics. I was mesmerised by the ease with which he discussed and illustrated the range of newly discovered subatomic particles. But when asked a week or two later to explain to a colleague what he had said, I could only recall fragments of his content and a few names. The fact is, that if I were to learn what he talked about, I would need to go back over the material several times before I could begin to see the underlying principles and structure, and to fit the details into them. That is, of course, unless I was a theoretical physicist who already knew the basic principles behind his talk.

The third main point is discussed in the next chapter. The aim of this discussion is to broaden our perspective and look at the role that peers play in the learning process.

4

CHAPTER 4

Life in classrooms: the contexts within which learning takes place

Learning within the classroom takes place within more than one context, within more than one world. As the evidence shows, the teacher is only one source of learning experiences. Peer interactions and social relationships are equally important and need to be carefully understood if student learning is to be explained and managed effectively. In the previous chapter, I described the learning process largely in terms of the mind of the individual student. In this chapter, I want to broaden the perspective and discuss the various worlds of the classroom that students experience, with a particular emphasis on the ways in which peers shape the learning process.

You will have noted that in the previous chapter, I described the learning process without reference to the students' intelligence or ability, and you probably saw this as a significant omission because we are used to assuming that student ability is perhaps the most important factor in determining what and how students learn. So what evidence about academic ability has emerged from our studies? I address this important question towards the end of the chapter.

The three worlds of the classroom

The examples and excerpts of student engagement with learning given in the previous chapters (especially the "food chain" example in Figure 3.3, Chapter 3) and that follow in this one suggest that students live their lives in classrooms within the context of three different, but interacting, worlds (Nuthall, 1999).

First, there is the public world that the teacher sees and manages. It is the only world that most of us see when we go into a classroom. In this world, the students (mostly) do what the teacher wants them to do, by following the public rules and customs of the classroom. This is the world structured by the learning activities and routines the teacher designs and manages.

Second, there is the semiprivate world of ongoing peer relationships. This is the world in which students establish and maintain their social roles and status. It has its own rules and customs, and students are acutely aware of them as they participate in the public world of the teacher. Transgressing peer customs may have worse consequences than transgressing the teacher's rules and customs. This peer-relationship world flows over into out-of-class activities, where clique formation goes on uncontrolled, and where adults do not usually see the teasing and the bullying.

Finally, there is the private world of the child's own mind. This is where children's knowledge and beliefs change and grow; where self-beliefs and attitudes have their effects; where individual thinking and learning takes place. This world, continuous over all aspects of a child's life, brings home life into the school and playground, and brings school life back into the home.

How significant are the three worlds in shaping student learning?

Each of these three worlds constantly shapes each student's experiences, and it is impossible to fully disentangle their respective effects. We tried to get an approximate indication by identifying when the students' learning is entirely dependent on self-generated activities or peer interactions. To find this out, we examined all the item files for the concepts learned in the Antarctica study. We then divided the item files into two categories.

First, there were those items dependent on teacher-managed activities. By this, I mean that the concept would not have been learned if it had not been for the experience the student gained from a teacher-managed activity. The teacher-managed activities were those activities in which the teacher was involved (for example, whole-class or small-group discussion, one-to-one talk with the teacher) or those set by the teacher and without student choice (for example, set written activity, required reading).

The second category included those item files in which learning the concept depended on a self-generated activity of some kind. We classified the self-generated learning experiences into three further categories. The first group (choice of teacher-designed activities) involved experiences dependent on a learning activity that the student had chosen from a set of alternative activities designed by the teacher. Thus, students could choose, for example, one of a set of readings, games, or other resources provided by the teacher, or they could choose one of a set of topics to investigate or write about. The activity each student chose was critical to that student's learning of the concept.

The second type of self-generated learning experiences (self-designed activities and use of resources) occurred when students were allowed to design the critical learning activity for themselves. Here, for example, a student might have added a section or drawing to a report, selected his or her own topic to research or write about, or done additional research or homework. In one instance, the teacher introduced the students to a card game designed to illustrate the food chain in Antarctica. Some of the students developed their own version of the game and played it during the lunch hour.

The third type of self-generated learning experience (spontaneous peer talk) occurred when the critical learning activity was a spontaneous conversation between peers. These conversations occurred during individual, group, and whole-class activities, but what particularly characterised them was that they were not required discussions; they occurred spontaneously and they arose out of, or in parallel with, required activities.

In many of the item files, we encountered more relevant learning experiences than were needed to learn the concept, idea, or principle. Where there were enough learning experiences during teacher-controlled activities for learning to occur, these were counted as being learned during teacher-controlled activities. Where there were not enough experiences during teacher-controlled activities for the concept to be learned, and the additional necessary learning experience came from self-generated activities, these were classified as self-generating learning experiences. (See www.nuthalltrust. org.nz for more information on coding the Project on Learning).

Figure 4.1 illustrates how often learning depended on teacher-managed activities or on self-chosen, or self-constructed, activities. On average, the teacher in this study provided a critical mass of learning experiences for about half of the concepts that the students learned. The learning of another quarter of the concepts depended on the particular teacher-designed activity the student chose. Because students could choose from a range of activities, the choice of activity determined what a student learned or did not learn. For example, the students were given a choice of which Antarctic animal to study. Many chose penguins—because they liked them and already knew a lot about them—but others chose whales and seals and learned more than they already knew. Finally, about a quarter of the concepts were learned through spontaneous talk, self-created activities, or use of resources. In other words, the students created their own critical learning experiences for a quarter of what they learned.

Figure 4.1 shows interesting individual differences. Paul's learning depended on teacher-managed activities for only 39.3 percent of the concepts he learned. At the other extreme, Teine's learning depended on teacher-managed activities for 64.5 percent of the concepts that she learned. Jim—the student who asked his peers about how to spell "Antarctica"—learned more from spontaneous talk amongst his peers (27.1 percent) than did any of the other students.

There were also marked differences in the extent to which the students learned from their selection of teacher-designed activities (see also the following section). Paul selected activities that were most likely to result in him learning something new. Jim hardly ever finished the activities he selected and consequently learned little from them.

There is another interesting finding buried in the data in this figure. Paul was the most able student in the class—based on standardised achievement and ability percentiles. He depended least on teacher-managed activities and most on peer talk and self-created activities. Teine was the least able (based on standardised achievement and ability percentiles), and she depended most on teacher-managed activities and least on peer talk and self-created activities.

Figure 4.1: The sources of critical learning experiences for students in the Antarctic unit

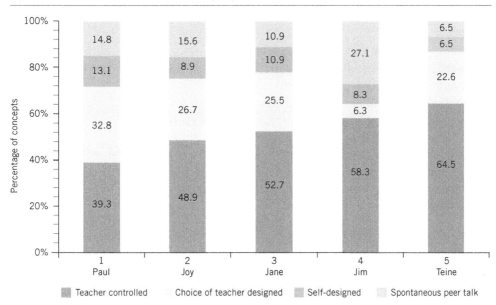

The influence of peer relationships

While it is clear that students continuously move between public and private worlds in the classroom, what is not often understood is just how powerful the social world of peer relationships is in shaping how and what students learn. In the following excerpts, I endeavour to illustrate some of the different ways that peers shape students' thinking and learning processes.

The first and most obvious examples relate to how students get information from one another. Exchanging relevant information (answers, procedures, directions) occurs very frequently in most classrooms whether the teacher is aware of this happening or not. The following example, featuring a Year 6 class studying ancient Egypt, illustrates the way a spontaneous conversation among interested students can contribute to the content that students learn. Adam, Dean, Judith, and Kenneth, working as a group, are looking through resource books for evidence of common occupations in ancient Egypt. Adam is reading about the life of the pharaohs.

Adam:	… Did you know when a pharaoh got buried, there was always a war over who would be the next pharaoh?
Dean:	Why?
Judith:	'Cause they didn't have a baby.
Adam:	Wonder what they done in the hospitals when they have a baby.
Dean:	Same thing we do here.
Judith:	They didn't have hospitals.
Kenneth:	The only thing that they had, they had midwives.
Dean:	Yeah I know.
Judith:	Oh yeah, the midwives …

The talk changes to a discussion of embalming, until Judith brings the discussion back to birth.

Judith:	They would have to go through all the pain, though, eh?
Dean:	What?
Judith:	When they had the baby.
Kenneth:	What? They don't have, like, sleeping pills back then.

In this exchange, Kenneth introduces the other students to another occupation (midwifery) that the others are not aware of and that might have existed in ancient Egypt. This conversation is more or less entirely spontaneous. It arises out of the interests of these students and their beliefs about life in ancient Egypt.

In the next example, the students in the Year 6 class studying Antarctica are writing a report on the talk given by a visiting speaker about her experiences in Antarctica. While the students work on their individual reports, the teacher does not discourage them from helping one another. The students talking in this example are sitting near one another at a cluster of tables. Jim wants to find out how to spell the word "Antarctica".

Jim:	(talking to self, but loud enough to be heard by the others) Oh! How do you spell that?
Koa:	What?
Jim:	That. Not the word 'that', but …
Tilly:	(teasing) T-H-A-.

Jim:	I said not the word 'that'. (to self as starts to write) A-N-T-A.
Koa:	What do you want? The word 'Antarctica'?
Jim:	Yeah.
Koa:	A-N-T-A-R- .
Jim:	(to self as he starts to write) T-A-R-.
Koa:	I-C-A.
Jim:	(to self as writes) T-I-A, I-C-A. Oops!
Paul:	You look over there (gestures to wall, where word is printed).
Tilly:	(inaudible)
Jim:	Oh, shut up Tilly! … I don't listen to dumb people.
Paul:	… and you look over there, and you look over there, and you look over on the board.
Jim:	If you don't shut up, Paul …
Paul:	(sarcastically) That's all the places you can really look unless, Jim, you look back at some of your own worksheets and your homework sheet even.

Koa is willing to help, but Paul is fed up with Jim always asking for help when he could help himself. In this case, the word "Antarctica" is printed in several places around the wall of the classroom, and Jim has used it himself in previous reports. Jim's sensitivity to Paul's and Tilly's comments results in him reacting angrily to both of them. Getting help from his peers is a minefield for Jim, who has limited reading and spelling ability. During this interchange, the students play out and develop their respective roles in relation to the knowledge needed to succeed in the class. The exchange confirms that Paul knows most of the required knowledge, that Jim is treated as a fool, that Koa is a helpful ally, and so on.

In the next example, Tui shows how he gets information from his peers. As part of a unit on the weather, the students have been directed outside their classroom to record wind direction and speed, temperature, and types of clouds. Tui tries to obtain the information he needs in the way he usually gets what he wants.

Tui:	(to Tim) What do the clouds look like, Tim? What do the clouds look like? What do the clouds look like? Want a hiding? Well, what do the clouds look like? What do the clouds look like?

A little later, he goes back to Tim to correct his own record of the wind direction. Tui does not understand what "wind direction" means. Is it the way the wind is going, or where it is coming from?

Tui:	Shit, I done it wrong. Wind. What way's the wind blowing? What way's the wind blowing, Tim?
Tim:	What way's the wind blowing? That way.
Tui:	The wind's blowing that way? That way's north? Eh? South? Eh? That way's south? Eh? Eh? Tim?
Tim:	What way's it coming from?
Tui:	I don't know. It's going that way. It's coming from the north. Yeah.

Although Tui tries to bully Tim, Tim deliberately plays on Tui's confusion, undermining Tui's authority and leaving him confused.

Within the social context of this classroom, Tui deals with his lack of knowledge and understanding by forcing others to provide him with what he needs to know. What he learns and how he learns it are a function of his social status, which he maintains aggressively out of the classroom and often also inside the classroom.

At the other end of the scale, students can facilitate one another's knowledge and play co-operative roles. The following discussion among a group of students occurs when the teacher asks them to list, as a group activity, as many words related to weather as they can think of. One of them suggests "snow", but Mary objects.

Mary:	No, it's not snow.
Glen:	Doesn't snow in New Zealand.
Jan:	It does not.
Glen:	Not in Christchurch.
Jan:	It only snows in the mountains.
Glen:	And Mount Cook.
Jan:	Yeah.
Glen:	And Mount Egmont and Mount everything.

Jan:	Mount Egmont I love. I've been over there. I've got a tee shirt of Mount Egmont.
Glen:	Mount Tekapo?
Jan:	Yeah.
Mary:	It just about snowed the other Friday. Last Friday. That was thick cloud.
Jan:	The clouds are, um ...
Glen:	Sheep clouds.
Jan:	Yeah. Sheep clouds, all puffy sheep clouds. Baa-lamb clouds.

One student's idea triggers another idea that triggers another idea. As a group, these students enjoy one another and one another's ideas, although the direction of the discussion has nothing to do with the teacher's intentions.

Dealing with disagreements

What happens when students encounter ideas that disagree with their own ideas? Tui tries to shout down the opposition, using his authority to insist he is right. His group is trying to determine, with the aid of a thermometer, the temperature outside the classroom.

Student 1:	(recording the weather for the group) What's the degrees [centigrade]?
Tui:	Seventeen.
Student 2:	No, it's not (taking the thermometer).
Tui:	Giz a look at that (reaching for thermometer). My eyes don't trick me.
Student 3:	It's 17.
Tui:	Giz it here.
Student 3:	Oh, it's gone down.
Tui:	Give it here or someone's going to get a sore mouth.
Student 3:	It's 16 now.
Tui:	Hold it up straight.
	(This argument continues for the next half minute.)
Tui:	It's 17. That's 15 there (pointing to scale on thermometer), so that's 16, and that's 17. OK? Got it?
Student 2:	It's 15.
Tui:	Get stuffed. (starts singing) Da da de de didi de ...

In contrast, Jim and Ben resolve their difference of belief by using evidence. They have been working together to produce a list of the kinds of occupations needed in Antarctica. Their list already contains the word "leader", and Jim suggests "guide". Ben disagrees, claiming that the role of leader implies the role of guide.

Jim:	Um, guide, guide.
Ben:	It's kind of like a leader?
Jim:	No, 'cause the expedition leader is a leader. He just, the guide knows where everythink is. The expedition leader doesn't. ...
Ben:	An expedition leader has to know where everything is as well or else he wouldn't be an expedition leader, 'cause he's supposed to guide them all around the place and tell 'em where to go.
Jim:	Yeah.
Ben:	He's the most experienced and therefore he should be the guide.
Jim:	Yeah, but first of all they'd need a guide that's been there. While he's learning ...
Ben:	Well, he wouldn't be the leader while he was learning.
Jim:	Yeah.

Access to resources and information

Regardless of ability, the girls often had less access to information and materials than did the boys. Elle, a high-achieving student in the Kitchen Chemistry unit, participates actively in whole-class lessons and in most group activities. But as she later tells the interviewer, she has little opportunity to participate when working with a group of boys.[5]

Elle:	That didn't work well because they were mostly boys. I was the only girl in the group, and Ned, he's quite bossy. Thinks he's pretty cool, so he doesn't really let other people have a turn at things.

During a unit on space in a Years 5 and 6 composite class, the teacher gives the students time to work independently on selected reading and writing tasks. Abby, a very low achiever, quickly gets a "Spaceways" poem book from the book table and sits down to read. Brock picks up the Spaceways book from her desk.

---

5 This information from Study 16 of Nuthall's Project on Learning is reported in Suzanne Collins' doctoral thesis (Collins, 2005, p. 371).

Abby:	What?
Brock:	We need this.
Abby:	I do.
Brock:	Oh stink, can we read it? Yeah, you're supposed to read.

Abby lets go of the Spaceways book, and Brock walks away with it.[6]

In an opening activity of a unit on the Aztecs, students in another Years 5 and 6 composite class are assigned to write open and closed questions, which they then try to answer through their reading. Ned, a lower achieving boy, tries unsuccessfully to get Jeff to clarify the directions for him.[7]

Ned:	Are you only supposed to do one question per page?
Jeff:	What do you mean?
Ned:	Like you write a question up and then you leave that page for all the things you're going to write down about it.
Jeff:	Miss H never said that, so …
Ned:	What?
Jeff:	Miss H never said that, so …

Unable to get a clear response from Jeff, Ned asks another boy, with no better results. Finally, he asks a girl and gets a definite—but incorrect—answer from Kirsty.

Ned:	Pat, are you supposed to do one question per page?
Pat:	I don't know.
Ned:	Kirsty, are you supposed to do one question per page?
Kirsty:	No, you just write down heaps of questions.
Ned:	Thank you.

Much student knowledge comes from peers

The important insight that comes from these exchanges is that much of the knowledge students acquire comes from their peers, and when it does, it comes wrapped inside their social relationships. Often, those with status know the answers

---

6 This information from Study 17 of Nuthall's Project on Learning is reported in Veronica O'Toole's doctoral thesis (O'Toole, 2005, p. 339). Veronica O'Toole participated in the data collection and analysis for the study.
7 This information from Study 18 of the Project on Learning is reported in Suzanne Collins' doctoral thesis (Collins, 2005, p. 253).

and control access to information and materials. Those without status are likely to have limited access to information and materials, have to ask for the answers, and may have to provide something in exchange. These social relationships change constantly, and students have to spend time in class maintaining and/or changing them.

The following example, recorded in the classroom of the Year 6 class studying Antarctica, takes place as the students work at their desks on an individual task. It follows on from their watching of the videotape cited in Chapter 3. The students are whispering as quietly as they can, and it is unlikely an observer would notice anything going on. The topic is the exchange of boyfriends.

Leigh:	(inaudible) if you want to get a boyfriend, get it down.
Teine:	Yeah, but it's not for me, I just … 'cause Nell said—oh, don't worry. But Nell wasn't planning. Nell said she was; Nell said she was trying to take John off you to give him to Maude.
Leigh:	Well, she's got no right to do that.
Teine:	Yeah, well (shrugs, throws sheet of paper onto Leigh's desk). Oh, no, I'll have to, I'll … tell Nell. I'll … What?
Leigh:	(whispering, inaudible)
Teine:	(whispering, inaudible)
Leigh:	(whispering, inaudible)
Teine:	What do you mean (inaudible) no, well, all … (starts singing to herself) 'Do you really want me baby?'

And so unfolds the world of the classroom in which much more than the curriculum content occupies the minds of the students.

The shaping of self-concepts through peer interactions

The concepts that students have of their own abilities and worth are constantly shaped by their classroom experiences, especially their interactions with other students. The process of evaluation that goes on in working memory is not just about the validity of the content of experiences but also about the validity (or ability) of the experiencer. This process seems based, in turn, on a process of constant comparisons as students hear others talking in public and private contexts and judge whether or not they could have said the same things or answered the same questions. Rata, a girl in the class studying the weather, did well in school but had difficulty believing in her own ability. In the example given in Figure 4.2, the teacher has been talking about how to read weather maps and has introduced the concept of "air pressure".

Figure 4.2: Class discussion on air pressure

Public discussion		Private talk	
Teacher:	What's another word for [air] pressure? Another way to explain pressure if we don't understand pressure? Rata?		
Rata:	How heavy the air is.		
Teacher:	Simple as that. Did you hear what she said, Sue?	*Rata*:	(to self) I got it right!
Sue:	No.		
Teacher:	Say it again, Rata.		
Rata:	How heavy the air is.		
Teacher:	It's the weight of air. What information can we use that tells us the weight of air? ...	*Rata*:	(whispers to peer) I didn't even know that was right.

Rata, like other students, evaluates her own answers (whether spoken or just thought) against those answers from other students the teacher judges to be correct. It is this constant evaluating that allows a student to know whether he or she understands and knows what the teacher expects. In the next example (Figure 4.3), Rata whispers to herself about her own thoughts. She has not spoken or written the answer.

Figure 4.3: Class discussion on mercury

Public discussion		Private talk	
Teacher:	What is the silver stuff called? Does anyone know?		
Student:	Mercury.		
Teacher:	Is that right? It *is* called mercury. No question about that. Used to be called in ancient times quicksilver. Why do you think it's called quicksilver?	*Rata*:	(to self) Good. I got it right then.
		Rata:	(to self) Cor, I got it right!
Student:	'Cause it's got silver in it.		

The next example (Figure 4.4) provides an insight into the world of peer relationships in which one student (Joe) appears intent on damaging the self-concepts of those around him. The example comes from a social studies unit on New York. One of the teacher's intentions for this unit is to help her Year 6 students understand how ethnic groups get into conflict with one another. The teacher is discussing migration to New York.

Figure 4.4: Class discussion on Manhattan Indians

Public discussion	Private talk to self and peers	
Teacher: They're called American Indians. In actual fact, they were called Manhattan Indians. White people, Europeans, were often wanting to get things that were valuable. Boats from England, or sailing ships ... Which Indies were they trying to get to, now?	*Joe*:	(to self) Madhattan.
	Joe:	(to self) Honkies.
	Jamie:	Oh. Shut up!
	Joe:	(to self) Honkies. Nigger. Black man. Samoans. They're going to play cricket, Jamie.
	Jamie:	Shut up!
	Joe:	Get stuffed, Jamie.

This episode seems to set Joe off, and a minute or two later, he starts to interfere with his other neighbour, Derek (Figure 4.5).

Figure 4.5: Class discussion of the founding of New York

Public discussion	Private talk to self and peers	
Teacher: I think it was the Duke of York. 1776. Why is that date significant, Caroline?	*Derek*:	(who has just been kicked by Joe under the table) Idiot! Get out!
Caroline: The American something?	*Joe*:	You kicked me first, you nigger!
Teacher: The American something? (turning to whole class) Thank you. We have got a lot of talkers today.	*Derek*:	Did not, you honkey tonk.
	Joe:	I'm not a honkey tonk. Nigger!
	Derek:	Honk!

Joe then tries another way of insulting Derek. This conversation takes place as the students move back to their desks after the class discussion.

Joe: (to Derek) Shut up you dick! God, you're dumb.
Derek: Prove it.
Joe: Now I'll prove that you're dumb.

Derek:	Prove it. You don't know.
Joe:	All right. I will. What's 59 divided by 16?
Derek:	You do it. I don't know.
Joe:	I'm asking you,
Derek:	Prove it.
Joe:	OK. I will. You dumbo. Nig nog. You do it. I'll kill you. Why not? You don't even know what one is, probably. What do you think one is? God, you're dumb.

During the next 10 minutes, Joe keeps on whispering to Derek at every opportunity, "God, you're dumb".

Perhaps what is particularly sad here is that Joe is the low-achieving student. But he keeps up this constant abuse of others, apparently without the awareness of the teacher.

We could explore much more of the fascinating world of the classroom as students experience it, noting the many different ways students affect one another's learning experiences and self-concepts—and the many ways in which interactions between peers shape the ways they interact with teacher-managed activities. But the examples given so far should provide sufficient insight into factors that shape both student learning and self-concept.

What role does ability play in student learning?

There is another important aspect of student learning that I want to introduce you to before completing this picture of student learning. When we learned to predict student learning by analysing their experiences, we paid no attention to their ability (as reflected in their standardised achievement and ability scores). We found that all the students learned when they had sufficient relevant experiences, and did not learn when they did not have those experiences. We considered the possibility that the errors we made in predicting learning related in some way to student ability. For example, our procedures might have underestimated the learning of the more able students, who might have learned from fewer experiences. Or we might have overestimated the learning of the less able students, who perhaps needed more relevant learning experiences. However, we found the errors we made in predicting learning did not relate in any way to student ability, which led us to conclude that student learning does not relate to student ability as measured by tests such as the standardised reading, listening comprehension, vocabulary, and mathematics tests. Since these tests, taken together, correlate highly with intelligence tests, they are good indicators of students' academic ability.

However, the picture now becomes more complicated. Although we could predict student learning without taking into account student ability, we found the more able students nevertheless usually learned more than the less able students did. They started with more background knowledge and so ended up with higher scores on the postunit achievement tests. Figures 4.6 and 4.7 show the test results (supplemented by interviews) for the Year 6 class studying Antarctica and for the Year 5 class studying a science unit on light. Each column for each student is made up of the items the student already knew (that is, got them right on the pretest) at the bottom, the items the student learned during the unit (in the middle of the column), and the items he or she never learned or mislearned (at the top of each column). The number of items each student got right on the posttest is the combination of the already known items and those items learned during the unit.

It is clear from Figure 4.6 that Paul had the most prior knowledge and knew the most on the posttest. Teine had the least prior knowledge and the lowest score on the posttest. The pattern in Figure 4.7 (for the class studying the science unit) is the same, except for Sonya, who, relative to her prior knowledge, learned more than could be expected during the unit.

These are the kinds of data we are used to seeing in the results of classroom tests, and the kinds we usually interpret to mean that students who are more able learn more than students who are less able. However, all our research evidence points to the fact that if both groups of students have the same experiences, the low-ability students learn just as much as the high-ability students.

There are several things we need to think about in order to make sense of this apparent contradiction. First, we should note in the following graphs that the results that we get on a test of learning administered after a unit (the posttest) reflect both what the students already knew as well as what they learned, and the largest proportion comprises what they already knew. In other words, posttests are more likely to reflect prior knowledge than they are learning.

Figure 4.6: Percentage of items already known, learned and not learned, during the Antarctic unit

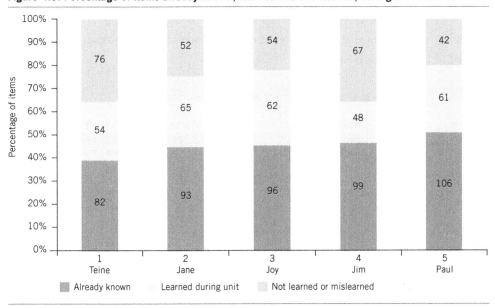

Figure 4.7: Percentage of items already known, learned and not learned, during the science unit

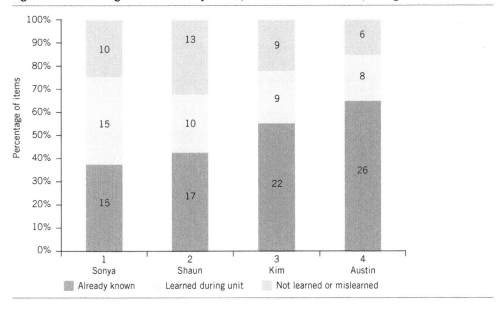

Second, what students learn during a unit is largely unique. Even though they are in the same class and apparently engaged in the same activities, what one student learns is not the same as what other students learn. Table 4.1 sets out the extent of this uniqueness.

Table 4.1: The uniqueness of student prior knowledge and learning

Student	Ability (average percentile on standardised tests)	Percent of prior knowledge known by no more than one other	Percent of items learned by no more than one other
Antarctic unit I			
Bruce	94	22.2	48.7
Peter	50	9.3	58.5
Claire	43	14.9	53.6
Ross	13	17.9	59.5
Teta	9	10.6	51.3
Antarctic unit II			
Paul	89	19.7	57.5
Jane	83	17.5	50.0
Joy	70	16.8	44.1
Jim	56	15.4	50.0
Teine	34	16.3	47.0
Science unit			
Austin	85	53.8	87.5
Karin	64	45.5	88.9
Shaun	46	23.5	80.0
Sonya	26	20.0	86.7
Social studies unit			
Jerry	73	62.1	65.6
Alice	68	50.0	62.1
Verity	28	38.1	84.6
Kent	25	51.9	65.0

The right-hand column of this table sets out the percentage of items that each student learned that no more than one other student learned. For example, during the first of the Antarctic units, slightly over 50 percent (48 to 59 percent) of what each student learned was learned by no more than one other student. This uniqueness was much higher in the science unit (80 to 89 percent). We could say that almost everything each student learned in the science unit was unique to that student and no more than one other student. Although student learning varies from class to class (or unit to unit), a great deal of what any one student learns is different from what other students learn. The data in the middle column of the table also show similar variations in how much prior knowledge students have in common, and that this uniqueness in learning does not relate in any way to student ability.

Third, there are considerable differences in how individual students make use of available resources and create their own learning activities. In Chapter 3, we saw in the example where student learning focused on Antarctica being the driest continent that the critical differences between Joy and Teine were as follows:

a. Teine getting involved in passing notes with her neighbours instead of attending to the video
b. Joy engaging in a group discussion about whether it rains in Antarctica
c. Joy choosing to write in her report about Antarctica being the driest continent.

The differences in each of these examples are apparently minor, but their accumulated effects are significant. One of the critical factors appears to be the background knowledge and level of interest that students have. In the following example (Figure 4.8), Nell, Paul, and Ben carry on a class discussion about what animals need to survive, but privately amongst themselves.

The teacher cuts off the discussion about surviving on water, but Nell, Paul and Ben have more they know and want to share. As Figure 4.8 indicates, such spontaneous talk often contributes to student learning and sometimes to significant student misunderstanding.

Another important factor is the students' understanding of what they are required to do. Frequently, because teachers rarely explain the learning purposes of activities, the students are most concerned about getting finished, no matter

Figure 4.8: Nell, Paul, and Ben carry on their own class discussion

Public discussion		Private talk to self and peers	
Kurt:	Could they, could animals just live on water do you think?		
Teacher:	OK. Well could you, could you just live on water?	Paul:	(to self) You can't.
Student:	No. You need vitamins and stuff like that.		
Student:	You can, but not for long.		
Koa:	You can, but you need solids and vitamins.		
Teacher:	Right. So you'd have a shorter lifespan if you just lived on water then would you?	Nell:	(to Paul and Ben, privately) It's five days.
		Paul:	No, it works in half days. Three minutes, three days, three weeks.
		Ben:	(inaudible) live for three weeks without water. Three days without food and things. No, no, no. Three days without food, three weeks without food, three days without water, three days without anything?

how. The key criterion is to take about as long, or slightly less, time than everyone else. Completing an activity too quickly might attract the teacher's attention. So constant comparison with other students' progress becomes important. The following example illustrates both this concern for finishing and the struggle for status that goes on continuously among low-achieving students.

Teine:	Are you up to Number 5?
Maude:	Yep.
Teine:	Fuckin' hell!
Maude:	I'm nearly up to Number 6.
Kurt:	I am up to 6.
Teine:	(to Kurt) Oh yeah, that'll be the day. (looks at Kurt's work) Oh yeah, you are!
Kurt:	Ah hah, Teine! Hah, hah!
Maude:	(imitating Teine derisively) Ooh, Teine goes, 'That'll be the day' and they go, 'Yeah,' and then she looks, and she says, 'Oh fuckin' hell.'

Many other ways in which students create and manage their own learning activities could be explored in this chapter. Some of the examples, given above, of the influence of peer relationships can be interpreted as examples of the ways in which students create and manage one another's learning opportunities.

Through this complex interaction of the teacher-managed and the peer-managed worlds of classroom experience, some students learn more than do others. This is not because they learn more quickly or more efficiently, but rather that because of their cultural backgrounds, their interests and motivations, and their skills in managing their social relationships, they create more learning experiences for themselves.

So what do we now know about student learning in the classroom?

The standard view of the classroom is that the teacher provides students with a set of activities. Some students do the activities well and learn more. Others do not complete the activities or do not do them well, and consequently do not learn as much. The assumption seems to be that all students experience essentially the same activities, and perform them according to their motivation or ability. So if a teacher is urged to use more open-ended questions, or to provide more positive feedback, it is assumed that this will transfer directly to all the students' experiences in much the same way. And it is also assumed that learning is the more or less automatic result of engaging in classroom activities. If students do what the teacher expects of them, follow the instructions carefully, complete all aspects of the tasks, then the students will learn what the teacher expects.

However, our research shows that almost none of this is true. Because of substantial differences in background knowledge and skill, because of differences in motivation and interest, and because of different peer relationships and status, each student engages in set tasks in different ways. Further, there is no guarantee that engaging in classroom activities in the ways in which the teacher intends will result in learning. Students need several (three or four) different interactions with relevant content for that content to be processed in their working memory and integrated into their long-term memory in such a way that it becomes part of their knowledge and beliefs. Because teachers do not normally design activities with this in mind, the effect is that individual students learn, or fail to learn, substantially different things from the same classroom activities.

I have always believed that most teachers are highly creative and resourceful when it comes to designing and managing classroom activities. Many do a very effective job of interesting and motivating students, and of managing student behaviour in the classroom. But in the light of this research, that creativity needs to be directed differently. The important factors that need to be taken into account are:

- the importance of differences in background knowledge and in the understandings and misunderstandings that students bring to any task
- the continuing power of peer relationships and status to determine what students do and how they evaluate their own and other students' involvement in classroom activities
- the need to constantly monitor what students are or are not learning from their activities and to respond accordingly.

If this chapter were not already longer than I intended, I would talk more about the ways students not only learn the content of activities, but also learn what they do. In the first chapter, I described how sitting in lectures teaches that knowledge is something we are given whether we like it or not. Students learn passivity in lectures. In hands-on activities, they can learn that what they find out for themselves is invariably wrong and that they have to be told what they should be seeing. The correct results of experiments are found in the back of the textbook. And so on. When we look at what students remember of their classroom experiences, we find the curriculum content wrapped up in the nature of the experience, which means that how students experience an activity is as much a part of what they learn as is the intended curriculum content. In fact, sometimes, memory for the task itself is longer lasting than the content the task was designed to teach. But more on this in Chapter 5.

Implications for teaching

This chapter should have made clear that peers are a major factor in student learning, even in the best run classrooms. In all the classes that we studied, the teachers used a mixture of whole-class, small-group, and individual activities. As might be expected, the frequency of peer interactions was significantly higher in small-group activities. But during individual activities and whole-class activities, there was still the constant presence of peer interactions.

This finding raises an important question about how teachers could and should most effectively manage a classroom. If a significant part of what a student learns is learned through informal, often spontaneous peer interactions, what, if anything, should the teacher do about this? Two answers have emerged in the research literature. One is for the teacher to become more involved in the peer culture and subtly work with it to manage each student's learning opportunities. The other is for the teacher to create a powerful classroom culture that overrides the natural peer culture.

Becoming involved in the peer culture

For many years, researchers have been fascinated with spontaneous group formation in schools and the ways in which students work out their respective statuses and roles. Questionnaires have been developed to allow teachers to identify the relative status and popularity of the students in their class. Students who trust their teacher and know that verbal and physical cruelty is not tolerated in their class can be quite open about their perceptions and feelings for other students. Teachers have been encouraged to make use of this information when determining seating patterns in their class, and when setting up groups for small-group work. However, this kind of information gets more and more difficult to obtain as the students grow into adolescence and feel increasingly insecure about who they are and what they can do.

Mehan and colleagues (for example, Mehan, Okamoto, & Adam, 1996) have done interesting research on the need to understand and work with each student's academic and social strengths. They found that classes in which academic achievement was the only criterion for success in the teacher's eyes tended to develop a fixed hierarchical peer status system in which the academically successful were always on top and constantly putting down those who were less successful. Classes in which a variety of different skills were emphasised, so that every student had some activity in which he or she could be the expert or leader, had a peer-status system with very little hierarchical structure, and very few established cliques (see also Morine-Dershimer, 1985). Although the peer culture is largely independent of the school culture, teachers can strongly influence it through the way they consciously or unconsciously award privileges and status.

Getting closer to students and their hidden peer culture raises ethical as well as teaching concerns. Elementary school teachers who stay with the same class of students through most of the school day are in a much better position to understand the peer culture than are high school teachers who work with several classes in any one school day. But how far should the elementary school teacher go? Students surely have a right to self-protection, which includes the right to an alternative culture within which they are safe from the teacher. How far should the teacher intrude on the most intimate aspects of their lives? These are questions that we can answer only when we have a much better understanding of the nature of the peer culture, how it develops, how it is sustained and what, exactly, it consists of.

Creating a powerful classroom culture

There has been much research in the last few years on the use of groups in teaching. Many of those who have attempted to provide guidelines for developing effective groups have emphasised the need for training students in effective group discussion and problem-solving techniques. What seems to have emerged from this research is that effective group work requires students to acquire a set of attitudes and beliefs. In other words, there is a need to develop the classroom as a learning community. But consideration of this enticing idea is a book in itself, and so unfortunately beyond the scope of this present small publication.

5

CHAPTER 5

How students learn from the variety of their experiences

The purpose of this chapter is to explore in more depth how students learn. In Chapter 3, I used the example of how three students learned, or failed to learn, that Antarctica is the driest continent. I cautioned that this was a very simple and transparent example. Most of the time, students' experiences are more complex and the information they come across is often partial or fragmented in ways that require them to infer connections.

In this chapter, I want to describe some of the complexity involved in students' learning in order to give a more accurate sense of how students' minds actually process their classroom experiences. In the third chapter, I described the experiences a student needed to learn a concept in the following way:

> … there is a certain amount of information that a student needs in order to understand that concept. This information might be, for example, a combination of a definition and a set of explicit examples. A student could experience this information in a variety of different ways, or in a variety of different parts.

We discovered that a student needed to encounter, *on at least three different occasions,* the complete set of the information he or she needed to understand a concept. If the information was incomplete, or not experienced on three different occasions, the student did not learn the concept.

This was a simplification of the full procedures in order not to distract you from the main purposes of that chapter. In fact, the procedures are more complex, as the processes that go on in a student's working memory are more sophisticated than this simple account suggests. The focus of this present chapter, therefore, is on how useful information from the variety of experiences that make up classroom life is identified, connected, and integrated in each student's working memory.

We found in our full analysis of the recordings from the many classrooms that students encountered relevant information in many different forms. Occasionally, students would experience all the information they needed to understand the concept or idea. This we described as an "explicit concept definition". On other occasions, students encountered information that did not explicitly contain all they needed to understand a concept, but from which they could (perhaps with help) infer or deduce what they needed to know. This we described as an "implicit concept definition".

Other forms of information provided part of what students needed to know, or provided them with explanations, examples, or background information. These other forms of information are those that are most common and that provide a better picture of just how students' minds process and learn from the experiences students have.

In the next section, I explore this range of different kinds of experiences and then, in the later section, describe how we incorporated these different experiences into our prediction of student learning.

What kinds of information do students experience?

Even though students may encounter a full account of the information they need, they do not always understand it. In the following example, a group of students is discussing the concept of "blackness" in order to answer a question about why a black sheet of paper appears black. Mary has read that a surface appears black when it absorbs all light, but she has difficulty understanding what this means.

Mary:	So how shall we put this in a sentence about the black light? (she reads from an information sheet) 'If an object absorbs all of the rainbow colours in light, no light is reflected and we see black.'
Austin:	If an object absorbs all the rainbow colours in light, no light is reflected and we see black. So … ?
Teacher:	(who has walked over to join them) What is blackness?
Mary:	I know. That's what I'm trying. I know what it means; I can't put it in a sentence.
Teacher:	It's very easy when you find it. What is blackness?
Mary:	It's like all the light together.
Austin:	It's um wait, it's. It's, it's, um.
Mary:	All the lights together.
Austin:	Oh, I don't know. Black is black (laughs).
Mary:	All lights together that are brought in daylight make black.
Austin:	Black is.
Mary:	If something gets, absorbs, lots of colours, no light will reflect, and you'll see black.
Austin:	So blackness is—wait, black is, blackness is caused by light. Blackness is caused by light being absorbed by objects.
Mary:	Being absorbed into objects, and the light won't reflect.
Teacher:	OK. What do you think now?
Mary:	Blackness is caused by, um, lots of colours all poured in one object.

In this episode, Austin and Mary struggle with the definition of blackness, trying to explain it in their own words. Mary in particular struggles with analogies that would help her understand. She starts by describing "all of the rainbow colours in light" as "all the lights together" and later translates "an object absorbs" into "all poured in one object". The words in the definition are being connected in her working memory to words (and ideas) she already understands. In trying to relate this episode to what these students learned, we put a query beside it to indicate that, although Austin and Mary had read and discussed why an object appears black, it was not clear how they understood this concept.

Another problem that students face is how to reconcile their differing perceptions and ideas. This is especially a problem when students are given an activity and need to interpret the results they obtain. In this next example, the students are looking at objects through red cellophane and are supposed to conclude that red cellophane lets through only red light. But when many people look through a colour filter, like coloured cellophane, their brains compensate and they "see" the original colours, tinted red, but still recognisable.

Mary:	The red [cellophane] lets through everything.
Austin:	Through the red? … OK.
Mary:	Something was able to get through the, um. The (inaudible).
Derek:	The blue; no, another colour went through.
Austin:	Yeah, but all of the colours went through. Depends how you hold it, eh?
Mary:	Yeah, all of the colours, depending how you hold it, all of them went through.

Austin tries to reconcile the students' different perceptions by saying, "Depends how you hold it", and Mary accepts this. Although the teacher intends them to learn that a red-light filter, like red cellophane, lets only red light through, none of this group of students is convinced from his or her own experience and each unintentionally misleads the others into thinking that red cellophane lets all the colours through.

So far, we have looked at examples where all of the relevant information has been available to the students. The problem they faced in these instances was one of understanding or interpretation. In the next set of examples, the students confront another kind of problem. They encounter information that is less than they need to understand the concept, or that relates to the concept in different ways. This difficulty means they have to store the information in their working memory and connect it to other incoming information needed to complete or clarify the whole concept.

The first example is of a situation in which a student has opportunity to infer the appropriate information. Expected to learn the meaning of the term "refraction", Maurice, Patrick, and Shaun are discussing an activity in which a pencil, placed in a glass of water, appears bent when looked at through the side of the glass.

Teacher:	(with Shaun's group) … What happens to the light when it goes through water? Who can remember?

Maurice:	It slows down and bends.
Patrick:	You read that out of the book.
Teacher:	Yeah, I was just going to ask you that. You read it out of the book, did you?
Maurice:	Yeah.
Teacher:	You're right. But I was just wondering; I thought you might have worked that out from refraction, OK?

Maurice and the teacher know that they are talking about refraction, but other parts of the recorded observation show that Shaun and Patrick do not. They could, however, infer that when light "slows down and bends", it is an example of refraction on the basis of the teacher's final comment. This may seem to be an improbable inference, except that Shaun and Patrick know they need to learn what refraction means, and they have previously been introduced to the concept. They need to make the appropriate connections in working memory between what they had already heard about refraction, and the beginning and end of this discussion.

In the next example, we return to Austin, still working on what happens when someone looks through a coloured light filter like red cellophane. By repeating the experiment (looking at different objects through red cellophane), he notices that all the colours have changed, except red.

Austin:	(talking to self) OK. Why I think this happened.
	(He writes in his book 'I think this happened because the red light [cellophane] doesn't change red but changes other colours.')

What Austin has done is work out for himself part of the information he needs to determine how a coloured filter works. When he adds this information to his former conclusion "all of the colours went through" (see above), this process leads him part of the way back to the correct interpretation. He now has some of the information he needs to fully understand how a light filter works. This information then remains available in his working memory, ready to be connected to any other relevant information he might encounter.

In this next example, Sonya is in the process of working out that a blue filter lets through only blue light. She is engaged in an activity that requires her to write words in different colours on a sheet of paper and to look at them through blue-coloured cellophane. She is in the process of borrowing a blue felt-tip pen to write a word in blue.

Sonya: (to Jake) Could I please use it after her? Thank you. No, I just need to try blue.

(Sonya picks out a blue felt from Jake's case and draws a small line on her card. She looks through the blue cellophane at the blue writing.)

Student: Does that one work?

Sonya: Yeah, this one works [is invisible].

Student: Could I use it after you please?

(She holds her card up for the teacher to see, and then holds her card up for Jake to see.)

Sonya: (to Jake) Look, you can't see it. You can't see what I wrote. Ha! You can't see what I wrote.

This activity does not tell Sonya that a blue filter lets through only blue light. Rather, it seems to imply that a blue filter does not let blue through at all (a blue line cannot be seen). As such, the activity requires considerable interpretation on Sonya's part for her to make sense of what she has discovered.

Sometimes the information comes in the form of an analogy, thereby requiring the students to see the connection between what they need to know and the analogy. In this example, the students are trying to find out how a rainbow forms.

Patrick: How rainbows happen. When rainbows fall through sunlight.

Shaun: (reading from an information sheet) No, when raindrops fall through sunlight, they act as a pris, prisms. (to self) Pris, prisms.

Fortunately, Shaun has already worked with a prism during this science unit and knows how to use it to create a rainbow-like light pattern on the wall. However, the use of analogies—which are common in classroom discussions—always presents the same problem. In this instance, Shaun needs to have his experience with a prism accessible in his working memory. He then has to interpret that experience to identify how the prism and the raindrop might be connected. Raindrops and prisms are both transparent and can glitter in the light. Using his background experience, Shaun needs to identify what it is about his experience with prisms that could be applied to raindrops.

Another kind of information comes from examples of a concept or idea. In this example, the students are learning that convex mirrors make them look smaller, and they are trying to think of examples where they have seen this effect.

Shaun:	(to Patrick) Where do we use curved mirrors? … Fashion shops, buses, boats, hospitals. Hospitals sometimes have them, eh? Mirror room.
Patrick:	Mirror room?
Shaun:	Mirror room. You know at carnivals and all that?
Patrick:	Have you seen—have you been on a (inaudible) in that old Farmers'store, how they have those big mirrors and they made you tall and thin and big?
Patrick:	That's about all [the examples], isn't it?
Shaun:	No, no, no, no. And going round, um, going, going round steep corners. Going round some corners.
Patrick:	Oh yeah, those big mirrors.
Shaun:	'Cause you know those corners sometimes, when you see them.
Patrick:	Oh yeah, if you went up on the hill.

The value of this discussion about examples is that it connects the concept (convex mirrors make us look smaller) to the students' experiences out of school. For Shaun and Patrick, the information about convex mirrors that they currently hold in working memory connects to relevant experiences they have stored in long-term memory. Making these connections ties their earlier experiences to a new set of technical terms (convex, light bending, and so on) that explains how curved mirrors work.

Finally, we have found that teachers sometimes use discussions to get students interested and thinking about a topic, without providing them with specific answers. In the following example, the teacher is helping her students think about what happens when a light is shone through transparent, translucent, and opaque objects. The example of an opaque object she uses is a book.

Teacher:	What happens to the light when it shines on that book?
Maurice:	It stops.

Shaun:	It stops.
Patrick:	It just goes whiter.
Carly:	It can't go through.
Verity:	It's too thick.
Patrick:	It just stays as it is.
Shaun:	Yeah, the book's too thick.
Teacher:	So what's actually happening to the light when it gets there?
Shaun:	It's stopping.
Patrick:	It's spreading out.
Shaun:	It's going smaller.
Patrick:	It's going bigger, it widens … 'cause now it's got nowhere to go through.
Teacher:	OK …

Each child now probably holds a variety of ideas in working memory that could be used to work out the required information (that light is reflected back off opaque objects). But further relevant information is needed for any of the students to make sense of this discussion. So, as in many instances of this kind, the students each store fragments of information in working memory, waiting for the further information that might help them integrate and make sense of those fragments.

A case study of processes going on in working memory

To explore further what goes on in working memory, I want to discuss an example of a girl learning about the meaning of the term "refraction". During this science unit on light, the students have to carry out a series of activities. Some of these are designed to help the students understand how refraction occurs. The teacher's intention for the students is that they understand the concept of refraction and the role it plays in a number of common experiences, such as how a magnifying glass works, what causes a mirage, and so on. I have considerably abbreviated this example in order to focus on the main learning process.

The first experiment requires the students to place a pencil in a glass of water, and to look at it from the side of the glass. The pencil should appear broken at the surface of the water because of the way the light travels differently through air and water. Sonya, alongside others in her group, carries out the experiment and draws a picture in her book of what she sees. Unfortunately, what she sees is the magnifying effect of the water, not the broken effect, so what she draws is that depicted in Figure 5.1.

Figure 5.1: Sonya's drawing of a pencil in a glass of water

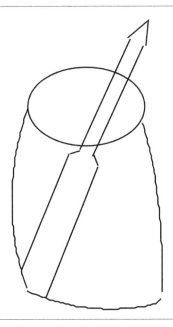

Sonya then reads her instruction sheet, which asks her to provide a description: "How has the shape and size of the pencil changed? Draw and label what you see." She writes underneath her drawing, *"What we did. We filled up the jar with water and put the pencil in on an angle. Half way down the pencil got fatter."* Next, she reads further down the instruction sheet, where it asks her to explain the effect she has observed. She repeats the experiment and writes, as she looks at the jar and talks aloud to herself, "Why we think it happened, because when it …" Her friend, Alice, sitting next to her, tries to help.

Alice: The water is a mirror.
Sonya: The water is a mirror?

Sonya: (starting to write "the water is a ..." and then asking Alice) How do you spell mirror? How do you spell mirror?

Sonya's completed sentence in her report reads: *"Why we think it happened. Because when it went into the water, the water is like a mirror so it makes it fatter."*

Two things are happening here. Sonya decides that the answer to the "why" question is the water in the jar. If not for the water, the effect will not occur. This is a perfectly logical answer, but not the kind of "scientific" answer the teacher is hoping for. Second, Alice introduces her to the idea that the shiny surface of the water is what is important. The surface is like a mirror. And what is happening in Sonya's working memory? Her perception of the pencil in the water connects to what she already knows about water and mirrors (for example, they reflect). She interprets what she sees as the result of the water: somehow, the water magnifies the pencil.

Shortly after this, Sonya is confronted by the difficulty of explaining something she does not understand. Her instruction sheet says that she is to answer the question: "What causes the bending of light (refraction) like you have seen in these activities?" The problem is that Sonya has not yet come across the concept of the "bending of light", or refraction. From other things she says, Sonya clearly thinks of light as a kind of pervasive substance that comes from the sun, surrounds us during the day, and goes away at night.

So, to understand this question, Sonya has to find a way of connecting her perception of the pencil and the explanation she has created about the water as a mirror to something called "the bending of light". Her response is to ask the teacher. But the teacher wants Sonya to work it out for herself and refers her to an information sheet that explains the bending of light. Sonya, however, does not seem to understand her. She returns to her desk and reads the original question again.

Sonya: 'What causes the bending of light (refraction) like you have seen in these activities?' What would cause the bending of light? Water caused the bending of light.

Kelly: Does it?

Sonya: Yeah, 'cause ... Oh, sorry. The bending of the light ... (she looks at the jar of water on the table) the water is making that look like that.

Kelly: (inaudible)

| Sonya: | No, but ... Yeah, the water is making the ... |
| Kelly: | Is it really making (inaudible)? |

Sonya seems to be dealing with the idea of "bending of light" by assimilating it into her previous conclusion that the water is the cause of what she sees in the jar. So the concept of "bending of light" (whatever, if anything, Sonya understands by this term) is added to the connections already established in her working memory between her perceptions of the pencil, the water, the mirror, and reflection and magnification.

A few minutes later, the teacher passes the desk where Sonya and Kelly are working. She asks them if they have read the information sheet.

Teacher:	(as she passes their table) Have you got the information sheet, you two?
Sonya:	(picks up the information sheet and reads to Kelly) 'Why light bends'. Here we go. 'Light moves more slowly.' Have you written this answer? 'Light moves more slowly through water than it moves through air. As the beam of light enters the water, it slows down and bends. As it re-enters the air, the light beam speeds up again.'
Kelly:	Speeds up?
Sonya:	'Speeds and bends back again. This is called refraction.' That's the answer! You've got to write 'Bending of light was caused by'.
Kelly:	Remember, she said bending of light ...
	(Sonya writes and talks to herself, 'Was caused by the water.')

Although Sonya reads an explanation of the bending of light to Kelly, and tells Kelly she has to write it down, Sonya herself stays with her original explanation and writes that the water causes the bending of light. Her reading has confronted her with a set of new concepts—that light is a beam that moves faster or slower, and bends. Instead of trying to make sense of these new concepts, she stays with her original explanation. Why she does this emerges in a later discussion.

A few minutes later, Sonya encounters another question on the instruction sheet that she has to answer. The question reads: "Find out about refraction. How is this important when it comes to the design of lenses for glasses, binoculars, and cameras?" Again, Sonya decides she does not know how to answer the question. The word "refraction" has come up before in connection with the "bending of light", so it is connected in her working memory with her perception of the pencil and the concepts of water, mirror, reflection, and the bending of light. But she can see no connection to glasses or binoculars. She decides to ask the teacher for help.

Teacher:	Right. You need to know what refraction means, don't you? Do you know what refraction means?
Kelly:	Yeah, when the light goes through and it bounces back.
Teacher:	OK. What's a nice easy way of saying what refraction means?
Sonya:	It bounces.
Teacher:	Mmm. What's another word than bouncing?
Sonya:	Reflect.
Teacher:	(referring to information sheet) Have a look at this sheet, and see what word keeps coming up again.
Sonya:	Bending.
Teacher:	OK, so what do you think refraction's about?
Sonya:	Bending.
Teacher:	OK, and you have to look [at the information sheet]. Here it is refraction, bending, isn't it?
Sonya:	Yeah.
Teacher:	Now, what was your problem? How is it important when it comes to designing lenses for glasses, binoculars, and cameras? How do you think that might be?
Kelly:	Reflect the sunlight (inaudible).
Teacher:	Is there anywhere in here [information sheet] that has anything about that [reflect]? No, there's not, is there?

During this discussion, Sonya has the words in her working memory (reflect, bending) and repeats what Kelly says ("bounces"). But there is nothing in her working memory that helps her connect these concepts to glasses and binoculars. So she and Kelly decide not to answer that question and move on to a question about the causes of a mirage. Sonya finds some relevant information and reads it to Kelly.

Sonya:	(reading the information sheet) OK. 'On a very hot day, you can sometimes see what looks like a pool of water on the road, although the road is really

	completely dry. Light from the sky is bent, refracted, by the hot air near the road and the sky. It is actually refracted sunlight. This is why people see mirages in a desert.' There you go.
Kelly:	Okay, so what is it? The sunlight.
Sonya:	Mirage is when you see things that the sun reflects.

Sonya writes her answer in her book: "A mirage is when you see things that aren't there because it reflects off the sunlight." The significance of what is in her working memory is now clearly apparent. The water–mirror–reflection–magnification set of connected concepts has remained central to her thinking and so she misreads "refraction" as "reflection", assuming perhaps, they are the same thing.

A little later, the teacher approaches Sonya and Kelly and asks them if they have finished. They say they have, except for the question about binoculars and glasses.

Sonya:	We're done, apart from Number 2. Number 2's hard.
Teacher:	It is, isn't it? OK, what does a binocular make? What does, what do binoculars do?
Kelly:	Make you see faraway things.
Teacher:	What do they look like to you?
Kelly:	Bigger and close.
Teacher:	OK, what do glasses do?
Kelly:	Make you see things better.
Teacher:	OK, what does a camera sometimes do? If I'm using my zoom lens?
Kelly:	Make it bigger.
Teacher:	OK, so how might bending of light help to make things bigger?
Kelly:	When it bends, it makes it bigger.
Teacher:	Maybe. You go and write it.
Kelly:	Yeah, when it bends, it makes things bigger. You have to write this down. Refraction is important to lenses.
	(Sonya writes in her book 'Refraction is important in lenses because'. She talks to herself: 'Because ...' then turns to Kelly: What is it, because?)
Kelly:	When it's like, its head is bent, it makes it bigger? That makes it ...
Sonya:	So is that the answer—it makes things bigger?
Kelly:	'Cause that bit of pencil that's in water is bigger.
Sonya:	Aye?

Kelly:	It makes that bit of pencil bigger than that.
	(Sonya finishes writing—'it makes things bigger.')

Between them, Sonya and Kelly connect the problem of how refraction relates to binoculars and glasses to their original explanation of the pencil in the water. Water reflects (refracts) and magnifies. Hence, Sonya writes, "Refraction is important in lenses because it makes things bigger." The water–mirror–reflection–magnification set of connected concepts in her working memory are used to explain lenses (binoculars and glasses).

Over the next few days, Sonya comes across the definition of refraction as the "bending of light" on several occasions. It becomes something that fixes in her working memory. But it is not until the sixth day of the unit that she encounters anything that involves her understanding of the concept. On this day, the group she is working with carries out an experiment in which they put their finger in a glass of water and look at it from the side. As they describe the results of placing a finger in water, the teacher asks them to explain what they are seeing.

Krista:	(reading the question aloud) 'Does your finger look bigger when it is in a jar of water?' Yes.
Sonya:	(looking at Jerry's finger in the jar, to teacher) Yes.
Teacher:	Why? …
Krista:	Because the water's like a magnifying glass, and it makes it bigger.
Teacher:	But why? What's that little …
Krista:	It's magnified.
Teacher:	Yeah, but what's that—oh no—see if you can think of some of the things you've done before now that might tell you why. It does magnify, but why does it magnify? Why does it make it look bigger? (leaves group)
Alice:	Because the air through the water makes things look um, bigger and closer up. And then it goes slowly, and it makes all the things in the water look close up.
Jerry:	Bigger.
Alice:	Bigger.

Sonya, who has been listening but not participating, has her belief that "water magnifies" confirmed. But she also hears Alice explain that it has something to do with air going through the water slowly.

A little later, the teacher returns to this group to check on their understanding.

Teacher: Krista come and help with this question. What happens to light when it goes through water? …

Krista: It moves slowly.

Teacher: OK. And what else is happening to it? Remember when you …

Alice: It makes things look bigger and, um, it bends them.

Krista: Fatter.

Jerry: It expands.

Teacher: OK, what's that flash word for bends them?

Alice: Refraction.

Teacher: Well done. OK.

During these two episodes, the water–mirror–reflection–magnification set of connected concepts in Sonya's working memory are strengthened by several references to water making things look bigger. She now knows this has something to do with light bending (Alice: "It makes things look bigger and, um, it bends them") and something to do with air or light going through water slowly.

When I talk with Sonya (about a week later) about her memory of what she did and learned during the unit, she recalls the experiment in which she placed a pencil in a glass of water.

Sonya: 'Cause, before when we were working in our groups, we did that.

Interviewer: You did that? Right.

Sonya: But I suppose it was just the water that did that.

Interviewer: It's the water. Do you know why it looks like that?

Sonya: No.

Interviewer: No. That's interesting. That's another of those funny things, isn't it, really. … So you remember that from actually doing it yourself?

Sonya: Yep. …

Interviewer: If you were trying to sort of think of why it would be like that, what would go through your head? What would you think yourself? Why do you think it might look like that?

Sonya: Because where the water ends, that's where the pencil breaks. So it would be something to do with the water.

Interviewer: Right. That's good thinking. What about the water is it that's somehow making it look like that at that point? … Any sort of thoughts about that?

Sonya: But when something goes in the water, the air moves slow ... Oh, I don't know.

Interviewer: Keep going. I think you're remembering something here. Something to do with the air?

Sonya: Mmm. And the water together.

Interviewer: And the water together.

Sonya: Yeah.

Interviewer: Now, I wonder where that thought came from.

Sonya: Oh, 'cause we were answering a question, and Krista was asking Alice, like, what did it mean, and she told us it was something to do with the air and the water.

Interviewer: Did she? So Alice you think ...

Sonya: I'm not sure who, someone in our group said something to do with the air and the bending of the light, so it makes the ...

Interviewer: Bending of the light, so it would ...

Sonya: So the pencil would go like that.

Interviewer: Wonderful. You've remembered something quite important there, I think. Still doesn't quite make sense to you though, does it?

Sonya: No.

What Sonya recalls reflects how she tried in working memory to integrate and make sense of her successive experiences with the concept of refraction. Initially, the process involved connecting new experiences to existing concepts. Sonya used her concepts of water, magnification—the pencil looking bigger in the water—and a mirror. These concepts brought with them their associated concepts—for example, water and mirrors reflect light. Once this network of concepts was established in working memory, it was used to interpret successive experiences. This process can involve developing and adding to the newly established network, or simply interpreting the new experiences as examples of the new network. In Sonya's case, she kept trying to assimilate the new experiences to her water–mirror–reflection–magnification–bending network. When she first read, "Light moves more slowly through water than it moves through air. As the beam of light enters the water, it slows down and bends. As it re-enters the air, the light beam speeds up again," she seemed to have ignored it in favour of her water explanation. Later, she read "refraction" as "reflection". But her final interview indicated there were still remnants of her experiences in working memory that had not been interpreted or assimilated into her network. She recalled Krista and/or Alice referring to air moving slowly and going into the water.

An underlying problem for Sonya seems to have been her concept of "light". Ideally, her network of concepts in working memory would have included the concept of light. But her understanding of light did not allow her to make this connection. Although she learned to repeat that "light bends", she did not understand what it meant to say light is a beam or light moves more slowly through water. Hence, she was not able to make the connections in working memory that would have allowed her to understand what she was supposed to be learning.

This analysis of Sonya's struggles with the concept of refraction should help clarify what lies behind the learning process in ordinary classrooms. Sonya's teacher worked hard to get the students in her class to understand the nature of light through a series of relatively simple experiments—looking at one's finger in a glass of water. She walked constantly round the class, watching each group and involving herself where she thought they had difficulties. As her interactions with Sonya show, she tried not to give answers to her students, but rather to encourage them to work out the answers for themselves. However, evolving misunderstandings are never easy to identify, especially when the students talk as though they understand.

This analysis should also help to identify the kind of work that a student must do as new experiences, new pieces of information, are encountered and entered into working memory. The first task seems to make sense of new experiences by relating them to known concepts. The second task is to hold new experiences in memory and to connect and integrate them with successive experiences that seem connected in some way. In the example of Sonya, I have removed all reference to the other experiences of other concepts that occurred during the unit on light. A full understanding would show that as she struggled with the concept of refraction, she also struggled with many other concepts involved in the other experiments the class carried out, for example, the colours of the spectrum, colour filters, how prisms work.

Predicting student learning

In this last section, I want to introduce the procedures we worked out for predicting what students would learn and remember from their classroom experiences. They are based on the kind of analysis of student learning illustrated through the example of students learning that Antarctica is the driest continent (in Chapter 3), and the example of Sonya learning—or not learning—about refraction. These formal procedures (described in detail in Nuthall, 2001) have been included here not because I think that any teacher would want to use them but because a general understanding of them indicates how we translated our understanding of student learning into relatively precise predictions. It will also indicate the combinations of experiences that produce student learning.

Once I realised that what students learn is a function of the kinds of information they encounter, I developed a system for classifying that information into categories that would help me understand what might be going on in their working memories. First, I separated out those experiences in which the student encountered all that they needed to fully understand the concept being learned. Then I worked my way through all the other kinds of information that might contribute to building up a network of related concepts in students' working memory. The following list provides an outline of these different kinds of information. It is based on a much fuller list containing many different subcategories and examples of how each occurred in different classrooms. Those of you who are interested can access this fuller list through the website nuthalltrust.org.nz

1. *Explicit concept definition or description*: The full information needed to understand the concept in words that a student can reasonably be expected to understand.
2. *Implicit or partial information*: Information containing some of the key elements but not all those required to understand the concept, or information from which an understanding of the concept can be deduced or inferred.
3. *Additional and background information*: Reasons, analogies, positive and negative examples, relevant personal experiences, definitions of parts of the concept.
4. *Preparatory or contextual information*: Indirectly relevant information; information about purposes, review of previous information, historical context, etc.

5. *Mention or uninformative reference to key words or concepts.*
6. *Activities and procedures*: Procedures that produce, create, or are intended to lead directly to concept-relevant information.
7. *Visual or object resources*: Resources in which relevant information is available but is not the focus of attention, for example, posters on the wall of the classroom.

Note that in this analysis, the term "concept" is used as shorthand for all the different kinds of knowledge and skills that the teachers wanted their students to learn.

The first step in the analysis was to determine, as best we could, exactly what relevant information a student encountered during a specific classroom experience. This process required us to discount experiences where the student was clearly distracted—for example, Teine passing notes and whispering during a video, in Chapter 3—or where there was evidence that the student did not understand the information available in the experience. We ignored the source of the information (the teacher, a book, another student, etc.—or the type of experience in which it occurred—listening to the teacher, carrying out an experiment, discussing with other students, etc. The focus was solely on what information the student encountered during an experience.

During my original analyses of individual student experiences, I found that students encountered two critical kinds of information. First, there was information coded under Category 1 above ("explicit concept definition"). I labelled that as Type A. Second, there was information that fell in the following categories: Code 2 ("implicit or partial information"); Code 3 ("additional and background information"); and (two varieties of) Code 6 ("any activity or procedure in which the item-relevant information is explicit and complete"/"any activity or procedure in which the part of the information needed to answer the item is explicit"). I labelled these types of information Type B. With reference to these definitions, I found that I could formally describe the information a student needed to learn a concept in the manner shown in Figure 5.2.

Figure 5.2: Rules for predicting which concepts a student will learn/will not learn and remember

If   A = Code 1 information

And B = either Code 2, or Code 3, or Code 6.1, or Code 6.2

Then working memory must contain either

$$A + A + A + A$$
$$\text{Or } A + A + A + B$$
$$\text{Or } A + A + B + B + B$$
$$\text{Or } A + B + B + B + B$$

This may all seem extremely formal and a long way from the classroom experiences of real students, but we needed to make the process formal in order to convince other researchers we were not being vague or engaging in wishful thinking. We needed to demonstrate that we could, in fact, predict student learning very precisely—that we had not overlooked any critical elements in the learning process. Table 5.1 shows just how precise we could be when using these procedures.

Table 5.1: Prediction success for concepts learned/not learned during the unit on Antarctica

Students	Number of concepts learned	Percent predicted that were learned	Number of concepts not learned	Percent predicted that were not learned	Aptitude (average percentile)
Jane	65	88	52	85	83
Joy	61	82	55	78	70
Jim	62	69	53	91	56
Paul	72	74	31	74	89
Teine	41	88	89	80	34

We can show what this table means by working from, for example, Jane's experiences. Here, we predicted she would learn 88 percent of the concepts that she actually did learn. And we predicted that she would not learn 85 percent of the concepts that she did not learn. In other words, in our predictions of the concepts that she would learn, and that she would not learn, we were right 88 percent and 85 percent of the time, respectively.

Two important conclusions

This chapter has been concerned with the details of students' learning experiences. I have moved away from the tidier descriptions of the previous chapters to the messy details of the realities of student experiences. If you have followed the descriptions in this chapter, you will have noted two things. First, students' minds are very busy making sense of multiple sets of concepts simultaneously during the course of a normal day's work in a classroom. Considered from the point of view of the number of concepts that become a more or less permanent part of a student's knowledge, the success rate, for all this mental work, is not especially high. Second, you will have noted that underlying this continuous complex processing of experience is a learning process that is not, in itself, especially complex. Provided a student is able to piece together, in working memory, the equivalent of three complete definitions or descriptions of a concept, that new concept will be constructed as part of the student's long-term memory.

6

CHAPTER 6

Ethnic differences and learning

A relatively small sample of students included in our studies identified themselves as Māori or Pasifika. In this chapter, I look closely at the experience of three of these students, both as individuals and as a group. You will remember their names from excerpts in the previous chapters, but in this chapter, I focus on their classroom experiences as a whole. Some of their personal details are set out in Table 6.1.

Rata, a girl who identified as Māori, was from the Year 5 class studying the weather. She was above average in ability as measured by the PAT tests (average percentile for age, 68). On the pretest, she scored 42 percent of the items correctly. On the posttest, she showed she had learned nearly half (46 percent) of the material she did not know on the pretest.

Tui, another student who identified as Māori, was also from the Year 5 class studying the weather. He was distinctly below average in ability as measured by the PAT tests (average percentile for age, 11). His scores on the pretest showed he knew very little of the content of the unit before the unit began (19 percent of the items), and during the unit he learned nearly a third (30 percent) of the material he did not know before the unit. Compared with the rest of the class studying the weather, Rata was better than average and Tui was significantly worse than average.

Table 6.1: Personal details and learning of the three students

	Tui	Rata	Teine
Age (years and months)	10.4	10.4	10.8
Average percentile on PAT tests	11	68	48
Percent of concepts already known before unit	19.0	42.2	38.7
Percent of unknown concepts learned during unit	29.8	45.9	41.54

The class that Tui and Rata were in was located in a lower working-class district with a relatively high proportion of non-European families. Of the 29 students in the class, 10 identified as Māori, two as Pasifika, and one as Asian.

The third student, Teine, was from the Year 7 class studying Antarctica. She was from one of the larger Pasifika nations. She was average in ability as measured by the PAT tests (average percentile for age, 48), but because she was the youngest in her class, she was lower than average in relation to the others in it. Her scores on the pretest showed she knew nearly 40 percent of the content of the unit before the unit began and learned just over 40 percent of what she did not know. In relation to her classmates, she knew and learned a little less than they did.

The class that Teine was in was located in a mixed working and professional class district. There were three Māori, two Pasifika, and three Asian students in the class, so the majority of the students were of European origins.

The story of Rata

Rata was a good-looking girl and a conscientious student. Although she got along with other students in her class, she had a limited social life outside the classroom. Her mother worked during the day, and Rata was required to go home immediately after school, where she watched television and did her homework. She was required to do housework on Saturday mornings (for which her mother paid her) and regularly attended Girl Guides. Her favourite activity was spending time on her uncle and aunt's farm looking after the animals.

Rata's attitudes to school and schoolwork seemed ambivalent. She said she did not like school but found holidays boring because there was nothing to do. She liked maths and writing stories, especially when she was allowed to write about animals. If she could choose what she did at school, she would do a research project on an animal, especially a beautiful animal, such as a lion.

Rata understood tasks better than most of the other students, anticipated what the teacher wanted, and acted as a leader in group activities. Although her group consisted of four students, she and Curtin did most of the work. She tried, however, to include the others, especially Mala (a Pasifika boy in her group). On one occasion, the group was completing a large chart of the different kinds of weather associated with different winds.

Rata:	Do you want to do anything, Mala? You can just help. Give us some information.
Mala:	What do I have to do?
Rata:	Help give us information.

Rata took responsibility for seeing that the group's tasks were completed in the way the teacher wanted. When her group was completing the chart, they found they had no data available on the weather associated with a north-east wind.

Rata:	Don't write anything out though, 'cause we've got to check it. Don't write, don't write anything. Don't write 'moderate breeze' all the time (as Curtin copies from another part of the chart).
Curtin:	But it was.
Rata:	Oh, God, dummy!
Curtin:	Well, you write it.
Rata:	Don't write 'moderate breeze' all the time. Shouldn't write the same thing all the time, as we'll get into trouble.

Rata constantly involved herself in helping others in her group. During class discussions, she whispered answers to Bruce and Curtin so they knew what to say. She explained things to the others, not always politely. In the following excerpt, she explains to Curtin how to use a hanging magnet as a compass.

Rata:	You want to know which way is north? Look on the blackboard, you nuthead. You have a little thing, a little needle, like this. No. You let it

go, and it goes away, and you know which way is north. It goes like this, and it points to the right way.

Rata clearly had considerably more relevant knowledge than did the others in her class. Some of this knowledge came from her home, where she talked with her mother and brother about school activities. She knew about the thermometer because her brother had one.

Rata: I like putting my hand on my brother's one [thermometer]—putting my hand on the bottom, and it goes up.

Other student: Does it?

Rata: Yeah. I like doing that. We've got one at home, and it's got the bottom like that, and I like putting my hand on it, and it goes up more ...

This understanding of how heat affects a thermometer allowed her to explain why her group got different temperature readings inside and outside the classroom ("Oh, no. I'll have to rub it out. It's gone up because we are in the heat of the classroom.") Later, to save confusion, she decided not to take the thermometer reading until the group came back into the classroom. None of the other students seemed to understand this.

A problem arose over what the students were supposed to do during the weather unit. Several students, including Rata, assumed the unit was the kind of "project" with which they were familiar. The work involved doing individual research on part of the topic and preparing a report (with pictures) for the teacher to assess. Because of the assumption she made, Rata found relevant books and spent time at home preparing her report. She urged her friends to do the same.

Rata: When are we going to do our project? Louise, have you started your project? I have. See, look, I have already started mine. We have to be finished by Friday.

Louise: This Friday?

Rata: I think so. We've already had two weeks. I've got more to do.

When Curtin asked what he should be doing in his project, she offered advice.

Curtin:	What should I do in my project?
Rata:	I don't know. Put 'What is weather?'
Curtin:	Types of clouds?
Rata:	Yeah, that's what I'm doing. I've got types of clouds. See, this book is good. See, look, it's got 'What is weather?' …

Later, when she asked the teacher about her project, he said that he did not expect anyone to do one.

Rata:	Mr A, what should I do with the project I wrote? I thought we had to do a project.
Teacher:	Keep it out. That's right. I'll take it anyway.

This outcome annoyed Rata not only because of the waste of time but because it lowered her status as a person who knew what the teacher wanted.

Rata:	I spent that time writing the project for nothing. See, Curtin, here's my project. We're not even supposed to do one.

Although Rata saw the project as a waste of time, it had a significant effect on what she learned about cloud types, weather maps, and other aspects of the weather unit. In the end, she completed a 12-page written report on a variety of weather-related topics, copied mostly from books she had read. Like other higher achieving students, Rata had created additional learning experiences for herself, independently of what the teacher required (see Figure 4.1 in Chapter 4 for patterns of other students).

Perhaps because of her background, Rata had a better understanding than many of her classmates of the class activities. Students often have difficulties knowing what they should be seeing when they are watching or conducting an experiment. Rata always knew the point of the experiments and activities during this unit. For example, as she watched the teacher turning a compass around, she identified the critical aspect.

Rata:	The needle in the compass, Sue, that needle always seems to point this way … I don't know. The needle in the compass always seems to point this way, sort of.

On the last day of the unit, the teacher set the very difficult task of predicting what would happen to a weather map over several days. Rata seemed to be the only one in the class who understood how to read the changes.

Rata: (to others in her group) What does it mean? What pattern is it? Starting from here (pointing to weather map). See, look, it's a pattern. It started off here first, on the coast, and it came here first, and it's gone right round New Zealand. See, look, it's pressure. The anticyclone starts off here, and moves up, and gets bigger …

However, despite her apparently clear understanding of what the activities were about and her engagement with each of the activities, she expressed ambivalent feelings about the unit. At times, she showed pleasure over what she was doing. When the teacher let the students work with a compass, she expressed delight ("Oh, cool. We're getting to look at it. First time!"). She was clearly annoyed about doing the project, and she commented daily to Curtin about how boring the activities were, especially the task of going outside and recording the details of the weather (wind speed and direction, types of clouds, etc.).

Rata: I reckon it's boring doing this. I reckon it's boring doing this day after day.

By the time we interviewed her, 12 months after the unit, Rata talked of definitely disliking school and what she had to do in school. Her attitudes seemed to be changing, as it was evident from her comments that the activities she was required to do in school were less and less to her liking.

The story of Tui

Although Tui sat within two metres of Rata in the same classroom, their worlds could not have been more different. Tui was also good looking, with a head of thick hair that he described as "fuzzy". He frequently wore a coloured band around his head. His father had died several years ago, and he lived at home with his mother and a sister and brother. His mother left for work every morning at 7.30 a.m., and Tui was free to spend his time after school however he liked. He seems, however, to have spent his weekends and several nights a week with an auntie and cousins. One of those cousins had run away and joined a street gang.

Tui's major love was sport. He played in softball, rugby league, and soccer teams for the school and for weekend sports clubs. About six months after the unit, he went on a tour of Australia with a representative rugby league team. The two things he liked at school were sport and art. In addition to becoming a professional sportsman (getting a black belt in karate), he wanted to be an artist when he grew up.

Through his cousins, Tui was in touch with street gang and Rastafarian culture. One of his foster cousins had given him a street name (Tavita) that he wanted to be known by.

Tui: You just make up your own street name. Just tell everyone that's your street name, and if anyone tries to get it off you, that's mine. It's just like street kids; they're mostly street kids, they've got street names … Oh, street kids, they like going on the run, and they like bombing places, and that … They all call me Tui, but I keep saying my street name is Tavita, and they forget.

Tui was also fascinated with Rastafarian culture. His favourite colours were the Rasta colours, black, red, gold, and green, and he used them whenever he could in class. He explained that:

Tui: Oh, Rastas are someone that's got a red and gold [head] band, and they're Rastas. Most of them have dreadlocks and that, and they belong to Māori gangs, once.

It was through his cousins that he learned about taking drugs.

Tui: Tony, we had dope.
Tony: What?
Tui: We had dope.
Tony: Where from?
Tui: This kid got it for us. You ask him. Kathy, we had dope last night, eh. And I'm, I had three of them. I gave one to him …

Inside the classroom, Tui often sang to himself, using the words of radical and protest songs:

There comes a time when we hear a certain call, when we all must come together as one, where all the people are one …

I can see a rainbow, red and yellow and green and black. I can sing a Rasta, a Rasta, a Rasta …

Kousta kinta, kousta kinta. Here comes the world. We are the world, we are the children …

What a rebel. Everybody say, what a rebel. Rebel …

During classroom activities, Tui was assertive in his relationships with others. He was usually active in organising how his group would carry out activities and managed to assign himself the nonacademic tasks such as printing and colouring headings. He identified two others in the group (Tony and Sue) as the main source of ideas ("Yeah, he's brainy. Oh, he knows how to spell long words like cumulus, and all this"), and often copied their work. Typical was the way he organised how the group carried out the task of preparing a large weather chart. The task was to divide the chart into four quarters labelled north-east, south-east, south-west, and north-west winds, and to describe in each quadrant the kind of weather associated with that wind.

Tui:	I'm doing it Rasta colours, OK? See theirs (looking at next group's chart). Theirs is neat. Theirs will be better than ours. I don't want that to happen.
Tony:	Don't worry about colouring it in.
Tui:	If we don't put in the information, we'll never get it finished.
Tony:	OK, then, well let's do it.
Tui:	I'm not writing anything.
Tony:	I'll write it down.
Tui:	No you won't.

Tui then helped get the information needed to fill in the chart. He went round the class, looking for a relevant book, found it, brought it back to the group and offered it as a source of information.

Tui:	Here, have a look at this book.
Kathy:	You get one square each [to fill in]. I'll decorate my square.
Tui:	I are. I are. Wait. I'm decorating them.

Kathy:	Do them in black and go round in blue …
Tui:	When we're finished, I'm going to decorate it.
Kathy:	I'm going to decorate my own square.
Tui:	No, you don't. I'm going to decorate all of them, thank you. I might as well just decorate it 'cause I'll be first. No, don't, you door knob. Oh you, shut up, door knob. You done it wrong, there.
Tony:	Don't put too much decoration round them words, 'cause you won't be able to read them.
Tui:	You will so. If you don't want me doing it, what are you going to do, door knob?

During this time, Tui managed to avoid adding anything of substance to the chart. While he decorated it, he ordered Sue to provide the content ("Start writing, Sue"). In most of the other group activities, he played a similar role, organising others with threats, and occupying himself in peripheral activities.

Threats and abuse were a normal part of Tui's relationship with those he worked with. He abused them and they abused him back.

Tui:	You are getting smart, Kathy. Kiss, kiss, kiss (laughing). Kathy ate duck shit. Kathy is black …
Tui:	(to student in next group whose surname is Daley) Daley bum. Getting smart, eh? Daley, you f ---, f ---. Getting smart. 'Cause you're going to get a hiding after school. I'm going to knock you to history …

Often the abuse was reciprocal, creating a climate in which abusive comments were freely exchanged.

Tui:	Hurry up. I need the ruler. Hurry up.
Tony:	Up your arse.
Tui:	Did you say, 'Up your arse?' Oh, well, that's all right with me …
Tony:	You're weird, man, weird.
Tui:	You cut that, man, or I'll break your face …

These kinds of interactions occurred several times a day and were an ingredient in the way Tui maintained his dominance over the others in the group despite the fact he knew less than they did about the purpose of the activities or their curriculum content.

Tui often followed his own idea of what had to be done, unaware of his misunderstandings. During an experiment in which the students balanced two inflated balloons on two ends of a stick, and then deflated one to observe the weight of the air in the balloons, Tui did what he wanted to do, and ruined the experiment.

Tui: What do you have to do?
Kathy: You have to make a hole in the top [of the balloon].
Tui: Here. I'll do it. I'll do it. You just get this. Tony, watch this. Watch this. That went down fast (pricking both balloons).
Tony: You were only meant to pop one balloon.
Tui: Well, we popped two.

Throughout the unit, Tui held on to his prior belief that the wind determines the direction of the needle in a compass. When the teacher discussed, with the rest of the class, how a compass worked, Tui focused on writing the heading for his individual project. When others offered reasons for the direction of the compass needle, he whispered to himself, "No, the wind's pulling it." When the teacher suspended several bar magnets on string to see which way they pointed, Tui urged others to blow them to make them work. He never listened at any moment when the working of the compass was being referred to or discussed, and continually confused the instruments for measuring wind direction and wind velocity.

Being wrong was something he found difficult to handle. Whenever it was clear to others that he misunderstood or got something wrong, he said, "I don't care, anyway," or started singing to himself and/or walked away. Tui was constantly concerned with his status and established a climate of threat against those not in his circle of friends.

Tui: Stella, go down to the park after school. I'll give you a hiding.
Tony: She won't turn up.
Tui: She'll turn up with her brother.
Tony: What does she want her brother for?
Tui: Her brother's a prick.
Tony: He's a prick?
Tui: We can get Stella when she comes to the Friday club. We could give her a hiding.

Two minutes later:

Tui: Stella, I can't wait till you come to the Friday club.

Six minutes later:

Tui: Penny, ask Stella who she's bringing to the park tonight after school to get a beating.

Tui's Māoriness was never referred to in any identifiable way in class. During interviews, Tui said that he would like to have learned to speak Māori, but he forgot the Māori words he learned.

Tui: …'cause I should have known them, 'cause I got Māori, a bit of Māori blood in me. I've learned Māori before, but I forget sometimes.

None of the members of his family knew more than a few words of Māori, but Tui was aware of his tribal connections and that only one other student in the school came from this North Island iwi (tribe).

Tui's attitudes to school and schoolwork were complex. In many ways, he tried to do well—but on his own terms. Instead of listening to instructions, he decided what needed to be done, often based on observing what others in the class had done. He completed activities but usually with the focus on the nonacademic components, such as writing headings and colouring and decorating. In the interviews, he never attributed anything he knew or had learned to the teacher or to class learning activities, and only occasionally to his friends in class.

Compared with the others in his class, Tui learned relatively little in the unit on weather. The problem was that, through his own management of his activities, he rarely engaged with the curriculum content of the unit. It is interesting to compare his participation in class activities with Rata's. Table 6.2 sets out some of the relevant details. The total time that Tui spent on relevant content was significantly less than the total time that Rata spent (724 minutes versus 882 minutes). However, because Tui knew so little at the beginning of the unit, he spent a relatively high proportion of his time on content that he did not know (92 percent), while Rata, who was more typical of other students, spent nearly a third of her time on content she already knew.

Table 6.2: Tui's and Rata's participation in class

	Tui	Rata
Total time spent on relevant content (minutes)	724.3	882.5
Percent of total time spent on content that was not known	92%	72%
Average time spent on concepts that were not learned (minutes)	7.4	7.10
Average time spent on concepts that were learned (minutes)	11.1	12.85
Total number of utterances recorded during the unit	1,064	2,077
Public utterances		
Percent of utterances contributing to class discussion	9.7	9.9
Private utterances to peers and self		
Percent of private utterances that were content related	38.2	42.1
Percent of private utterances that were task related	28.0	27.2

When we look at how much Tui spoke during the unit, we can see that he spoke only half as often as Rata (1,064 utterances versus 2,077). The kinds of talk he engaged in were proportionately the same as the kinds of talk Rata engaged in, but they occurred half as often. However, the learning process for Tui was the same as the learning process for Rata. Learning a new concept for him required the same set of experiences as it did for Rata. As the evidence in Table 6.2 indicates, the two children spent approximately the same amount of time (average minutes per concept) on concepts they learned (11.1 and 12.9 minutes) and on concepts they did not learn (7.4 and 7.1 minutes). The difference was in the way Tui managed his participation in relevant classroom learning activities during the weather unit.

In contrast, Tui did well in mathematics. He was very proud of the fact that he had learned all the tables. When he was asked about why he liked maths, he said:

Tui: Aw, I just wanted to be good at one subject, and I chose maths.
Interviewer: What's the problem with reading?
Tui.   Not that brainy. In my maths, I got nearly all mine right, and that. I try hard for maths.
Interviewer: If you tried harder at reading, would you do better?
Tui: Probably.

Again, it seems that Tui decided what he wanted to do and ignored or failed to understand what the teacher wanted him to do. In a way, he made the school his own, taking a leadership role—through threats of violence—and succeeding, in his own terms, to complete the activities required of him. But the exciting world for him was outside the classroom—a world of Rambo videos, karate, success at sport, cousins who became street kids, dope, Rastafarian colours, Rastafarian graffiti and dreadlocks, and connections to Māori gangs.

The story of Teine

Teine was born in one of the larger Pasifika nations. An active girl, with a shock of black hair, she preferred sport to school, but did not dislike school. She was the youngest student in her class and thought going to this intermediate school would be difficult, but had not found it hard so far.

Teine lived at home with her parents and an older sister. She did not speak her parents' first language, and they did not speak it to her, but did speak it between themselves. Teine had been back to her home island several times and stayed with relatives in a village shop. Others of her family lived close by, and when her parents were out at night—which was frequently—an uncle and grandmother looked after Teine and her sister.

Teine played netball and softball for the school and for weekend sports clubs. At the time we interviewed her, she was actively involved in playing competitive touch football for a church-based team called the Beulah Angels. Her favourite sport, however, was volleyball, which she also played competitively for a sports club.

Inside the class, Teine was an active and inquiring student. When she did not understand something, she never hesitated to ask the teacher or her classmates. She contributed actively to both whole-class discussions and her small-group discussions. During a brainstorm of words about Antarctica on the second day of a unit on Antarctica, she contributed igloos, sperm whales, snowmobiles, blubber, and explorers. She provided two of her neighbours with further words by whispering to them. When the teacher asked another neighbour, Nathan, to name an explorer, she whispered the name of "Ross" to him.

Teine often took responsibility with Leigh for the effective working of her group. On the third day of the unit, the members of her group were required to write a summary of a story ("Fire and Ice") they had read. In the following excerpt from this activity, Jan is writing and Teine and Leigh are suggesting what she should write. The two boys in the group (Jim and Nathan) fool around and contribute nothing.

Teine: (to Jim and Nathan) We'll separate you guys. (to Jan and Leigh) The story's about, is about a lady named Kathy ... called Kathy, Katherine ... They were explorers. And how she got the opportunity ... opportunity to go to Antarctica.

Nathan: (in a parallel conversation about the same story) 'Fire and Ice'. Usually you make fire out of oil, but they made fire out of ice.

Jim: Right!

Nathan: Talk about winners.

Jim: Next they'll be making fire out of water.

Nathan: Probably make fire out of you (making explosive noise)! It would just go whoosh!

At this point, Jim and Nathan re-enter the group's conversation.

Jim: Now, I know what happened [in the story].

Leigh: What?

Jim: Um, well, the other people they, they went and they made heaps, and ...

Nathan: He doesn't know what he's talking about.

Jim: Exactly. You hit it right on the forehead (play punches Nathan's forehead).

Jim adjusts Teine's pencil case on Teine's desk to where Nathan (accidentally) nudges it, so it falls on the floor. Teine responds by hitting Jim.

Teine: Oh, stop it you guys!

Jim: Oow! (to Leigh) I did nothink!

Leigh: Jim, you're going to have to, we'll have to shift you if you're not going to be quiet.

Teine: We'll separate you guys.

Nathan: Nah ...

Teine:	(to Jim) Next time, shut up then. Don't get smart. (to Nathan, sarcastically) You're so funny.
Jan:	They're trying to be stupid 'cause they think they're so funny.
Teine:	(resuming the summary of the story) Hey, look. It says Kathy and her travelling companion Paddington Bear.
Nathan:	I could have told you that.
Leigh:	Oh, wow! Why didn't you then?
Nathan:	'Cause Teine didn't read it out in time.

Jim takes Teine's copy of the story.

Teine:	Do you mind!

Teine hits his hand lightly and grabs the reading back. Jim hits her twice as hard with his fist.

Jim:	Yeah, I do mind!
Teine:	Oh, you missed! You got the paper.
Leigh:	Stop fighting, you two!
Jim:	It's her.
Teine:	It's you! Do something useful for once. (to teacher who is passing) Can you tell them to stop being stupid?

It is clear from this exchange that Teine could give as good as she got from the boys as she tried to focus, with Leigh and Jan, on the purpose of the task. This quality of aggressive social interaction was an apparent characteristic of the groups in which Teine worked. There was a constant competitive interaction between Teine and Leigh. On the second day of the unit (the day before the above exchange), the teacher asks the members of the class to work individually, writing down all the words they could think of about Antarctica, at which point Teine looks inside Leigh's desk for something, and Leigh hits her hand.

Teine:	I was just looking for the thing. (Leigh hits her again) I thought you … Oh!

Teine spreads her hands out and bangs them down on her desk in frustration. A little later, Teine screws up the piece of paper she has been writing on.

Leigh:	Teine. Be quiet!

143

Teine laughs as she throws the piece of paper on the floor and ducks a hit from Leigh. Later, as the teacher writes the brainstorm words on the blackboard, Leigh complains that Teine is not taking notes.

Leigh: (sighing) You're not writing them down.

Teine: (starting writing) Don't worry.

Leigh snatches Teine's pen from her. This competitive interaction then extends to others in their group. Teine complains to Leigh that Colin cannot spell the word "penguin".

Teine: (pointing to Colin's work) Ooh, ooh, he can't even spell.

Cory: Who?

Teine: Colin. He can't spell 'penguin'. He goes P-E-G-U-N-I.

Leigh: Teine, some people aren't good at spelling.

Teine: (to Leigh) OK. I shouldn't have said it in front of you.

Leigh: I know that.

Cory: Teine, you think you're good at everything.

Nathan: (to Teine, looking at her work) *You* spelt 'penguin' wrong. You forgot to put in the 'N'.

Leigh: Hah, hah!

A little later, Cory and Nathan again attack Teine's spelling. They are writing about Lake Tekapo in their report. Cory asks Teine how to spell "Tekapo".

Teine: (to Cory) It's T-E-K-O …

Cory: It's T-E-A-K in Māori spelling.

Teine: Yeah.

Nathan: So much for your brilliant spelling, Teine.

Teine: So much for your wimping!

Nathan: (inaudible)

Teine: Oh, shut up!

Teine later reported that, unlike the other girls, she did not mind working with boys. Where the other girls found boys annoying, she seemed to enjoy interacting with them on their terms.

Kurt: Yeah, I'll beat him [Colin] up after school.

Cory: Oh, you couldn't.

Nathan:	Yeah, sure Teine.
Teine:	Yeah, I can. When I, when I get angry.
Nathan:	Sure.
Teine:	I can! When I get angry, I get really angry, eh?
Kurt:	I think I could strangle him.
Teine:	Hey, I can beat Colin up, eh? At [previous school] I got really angry with Justin, and I punched him in the face, and he started bleeding.

While Teine managed her involvement in classroom learning activities reasonably effectively, she was also concerned with sustaining her social involvement with the girls in the class. Although she was significantly younger than they were, she participated in their private discussions about boys as boyfriends. The example of learning about Antarctica as the driest continent (in Chapter 3) showed Teine passing notes about boyfriends to Leigh and Abbie when she should have been watching a video. These conversations about boyfriends continued throughout the unit. The following excerpts are not complete because they were whispered conversations that even the personal microphones could not pick up clearly.

Leigh:	If you want to get a boyfriend, get (inaudible).
Teine:	Yeah, but it's not for me, I just … (inaudible). 'Cause Nell said, oh, don't worry. But Nell wasn't planning. Nell said she was trying to take John off you to give him to Maude.
Leigh:	Well, she's got no right to do that.
Teine:	Yeah, well. I'll have to, I'll tell Nell. I'll … What? (sings to herself) 'Do you really want me, baby?'
Leigh:	(inaudible).
Teine:	Yeah, well Abbie, well Abbie's … I know 'cause she's too shy. Everyone's teasing her about, she likes Colin, which is, I think is true.
	(Teine receives a note from Leigh. She reads the note, writes on the note, and passes it to Abbie.)
Teine:	(to Abbie) If you want him, you can have him.
Leigh:	Pride. Is that the way you think she's going to act? Just try to be mature about this.
Teine:	Yeah, I know, but if she wants John—I mean she never acts as if she wants him. You know, like I was …
Leigh:	With his name written all over her pencil case? …

At other times, Teine maintained her interest in reading by reading books surreptitiously under her desk. On several days of the unit, she read a book of horror stories whenever she could. The observer noted on the second day:

> Teine takes out and reads horror book under desk for a minute, then covers it with her pad. Later, when the teacher discussed the video with class: Teine returns to reading horror book beneath desk for about a minute. Raises hand from time to time. Covers book with pad as observer passes. Goes back to reading horror book. Raises hand. Becomes involved in the class discussion. Teine goes back to reading horror book. Reads it for three and a half minutes, glancing up from time to time. Puts book back in desk.

Then, on the fifth day of the unit, the observer noted that when the rest of the class were writing a report, Teine opened her desk and took out her book.

Teine: (talking to self) I'm going to read this till I'm finished with it.

Teine read her book of horror stories for another 10 minutes.

The issue of Teine's ethnic background came up in different ways. During our interviews, I asked her in several ways if being a Pasifika person affected how others liked her or interacted with her. She always said it didn't. But her background did come up in class, as in the following example when her group was discussing sharks.

Kurt: They're cold blooded. And they like shallow water.
Teine: Yeah, they do.
Robin: They like warm water?
Teine: Yeah, they do. In Samoa, the sun shines on the sea, and you can see some sharks.
Kurt: (laughing and exaggerating Teine's accent) In Samoa, the sun shines on the sea.
Teine: (tries to slap Kurt)

Other times when Teine referred to her country of origin, the other students simply ignored her. So long as she talked about things that were part of their common experience, she seemed an integral part of the social group, but the moment her unique experiences came up, the conversations stopped.

Teine: Oh, I had a snake in Samoa. It was really cool.

Maude and Jill, who had been working with her, ignored what she said and continued what they were doing.

Teine reserved her sharpest comments for a boy in the class who came from the same Pasifika nation. He had limited understanding of English, and the teacher went out of her way to include him in discussions, much to Teine's embarrassment. On one occasion, as the class discussed a talk given by a visiting scientist, the teacher asked Lapana to contribute.

Teacher:	Right. Lapana?
Lapana:	(smiling) Um, I dunno.
Teacher:	What did you think of the clothing? Did you think that they would have to wear so much clothing?
Lapana:	Yeah.
Teacher:	You did? You thought that they would have to wear all that gear?
Teine:	(whispering to herself) Oh, dick! Stupid idiot! Doesn't even know!
Teacher:	Would you wear that if you were in Christchurch?
Lapana:	I dunno.

In contrast, Teine seemed fascinated with students who seemed to know a lot. She was particularly interested in Ben, who was credited by his peers as knowing more than anyone else. She enjoyed playing word games with him.

Teine:	Dickhead. Where? Where does it say it?
Ben:	Yeah. There's no such thing as 'dick' in the dictionary; therefore it cannot be used.
Teine:	Look, you just said 'dick'. In 'dictionary'.
Ben:	That is a weak pun.

Another time, she asked him how he knew so much, as though his knowledge was a mystery she wanted to uncover. She seemed to see him as someone from a distinctly different culture.

Teine:	How come you know so much?
Ben:	Oh, I read a lot of books.
Teine:	Have you got a sister? How many? One sister? Any brothers? Just one sister?
Ben:	I've got ... (inaudible).

She then tried to draw him into the gossip about boyfriends and girlfriends. Ben had no interest in this gossip at all.

Teine:	Do you like Sally?
Ben:	Heck no!
Teine:	Sally told me that.
Ben:	Why would she get it into her head that I like her? (inaudible)
Teine:	I know, 'cause she's crazy about you.

Teine also seems to have been aware that other students were ostracised by the majority in the class. During the interview, she reported that her friend, Leigh, hated Shannon. When I asked why, she explained:

Teine:	Because there's rumours. That's why the girls don't want him in the group. People say that he's poor, and that's why Leigh doesn't like him. That's all.

She also explained that generally the girls did not like the boys in the class:

Teine:	'Cause they're always pestering them.
Interviewer:	What sort of pestering?
Teine:	Like, putting them down.
Interviewer:	Do they put you down?
Teine:	Oh, no!

All this evidence suggests that Teine coped well with being a member of an ethnic minority group. Whenever anyone tried to put her down, she reacted aggressively in a manner similar to her nonminority peers. She was aware she had a different experience from her peers, and she was acutely embarrassed that another student from the same background was apparently "dumber" than the others, but she seemed to treat herself and her peers as social equals. They were competitive, sometimes aggressive, constantly ready to retaliate for any put-downs, but without fixed or culturally based antagonisms. The subjects of their sharp reactions one day were their allies the next.

The role of ethnicity in these classrooms

Those who remember the article that Adrienne Alton-Lee, John Patrick and I wrote in 1987 titled "Take Your Brown Hand off My Book" (Alton Lee, Nuthall, & Patrick, 1989) will know that, in two of our studies, we found evidence of racial prejudice in the interactions between students. In one study, the teacher used an investigation of the ethnic diversity of New York to help his students understand the need for ethnic sensitivity and tolerance. It was in this study that we found evidence of continual ethnic abuse among students, outside the awareness of the teacher. It was as though the teacher's introduction of ethnic issues during the topic provided a stimulus for ethnic abuse to develop between the students. We noted an unconscious use of the "we" and "them" pronouns by both the teacher and the students. When Europeans were referred to, the inclusive pronoun "we" was used. When non-Europeans were referred to, the distancing pronoun "them" was used. The hidden assumption was that "we" in the class were all of European origin, distinct from other ethnic groups and cultures.

There is no direct evidence of direct racial abuse in the experience of the three students we have just encountered. In Teine's class, the teacher worked hard to be inclusive. Each morning, the students greeted one another with greetings in the languages of their ethnic origins. The teacher used a series of Māori phrases for managing the class and getting their attention when she wanted it.

In Rata and Tui's class, there was no evidence that the teacher included, or made use of, Māori culture. Despite a range of ethnic differences in the class, the curriculum did not include any aspects of non-European cultures. The teacher believed the students in his class, because of their working-class origins, needed help to think of the future, hence his idea that teaching them about weather forecasting would be socially helpful. It seems likely that if the teacher had included Māori concepts related to the weather and the elements, Tui would have been much more interested and involved. This inclusion could possibly have provided the bridge between the culture of the school and the culture of his home and extended family.

Each of these three students lived on the margins of two cultures—the culture of their homes and their extended families, and the culture of the school and its curriculum. They also each lived within a third culture—the culture of their peers. Each of the three students appeared to be managing their involvement within their peer culture relatively effectively. They participated, in different ways, in leadership activities in their working groups: Tui, through threats of aggression; Rata through taking responsibility and knowing more; and Teine through her own shrewdness and social skills.

However, they differed in how they managed their marginal status between the school culture and the culture of their homes and families. Rata was succeeding well in school. She had internalised the expectations of the teacher and appeared to receive support in her schoolwork from her mother and brother. Tui made clear his strong pull towards the culture of his cousins and their friends. This culture was an alternative one of street kids, Rastafarians, and gang-style aggression. He managed his participation in the school culture with limited interest and personal involvement. He tried to save face by getting others to help him complete reports, and by selecting one subject (mathematics) on which to focus his ability. Teine, like Rata, seemed to be doing relatively well within the school culture. Her extensive reading helped her sustain the knowledge she needed to cope with school learning tasks. But her various attempts to sustain her peer-group relationships were not helping her involvement in the school culture. Where other girls in her class focused their abilities and anxieties on doing well in the learning activities, Teine was tempted to match the boys in their active avoidance of school tasks, and engage the girls in their evolving interest in boyfriend–girlfriend relationships.

Compared with other students in the class who also came from homes and families where the culture was very different from the school culture, these Māori and Pasifika students did not seem to face significantly greater difficulties. Within the context of a city where Māori and Pasifika cultures were not strongly visible or the source of public debate, the cultural divide between ethnic minority students and majority students did not seem qualitatively different from the cultural divide between students from very low-income homes and students from average- and higher income homes.

This is not to belittle the effects of cultural differences on the school achievement of students. The pull of alternative cultures can be very strong and can result in students abandoning their attempts to succeed in school as their allegiance to the alternative culture (with its different values and goals) grows more powerful. It is not difficult to predict that Tui's future will most closely align with the alternative culture of the street.

One final warning may be in order. Close examination of the classroom experiences of these students suggests that, in their own way, they are coping well with life in the classroom. They have achieved status and know how to manage their classroom activities in ways they find satisfactory. If, for example, a teacher were to introduce Māori culture into the curriculum, and it had the effect of calling attention to the differences of the Māori children in class, it could change the balance of power between the children, not necessarily for the better. The content of the curriculum can have a direct effect on the status and roles of individual children, and sometimes in unpredictable ways.

CHAPTER 7

Teaching for learning: a summary

Ian Wilkinson and Richard Anderson

If we are to understand how teaching relates to learning, we have to begin
at the closest point to that learning, and that is students' experience.

(Graham Nuthall, Jean Herbison lecture, New Zealand Association for Research in
Education Conference, Christchurch, 2001)

We suspect that as you read the preceding chapters, you found you already
knew much of what you encountered. Some of you probably knew that scores on
standardised tests tell you only a little more about your students' learning than you
know already. Some of you probably knew there is more to teaching than simply
engaging students in activities. Some of you probably knew how important it is
to give students opportunities to revisit concepts you want them to learn. And
some of you probably knew that peer culture has a powerful influence on students,
especially on students in middle school. Of course, and as we have learned from
Graham Nuthall's work, the prior knowledge that you brought to bear when
reading those chapters will have differed radically from the prior knowledge other

readers brought to them. Nevertheless, you, and those other readers, probably already knew quite a lot before reading this book.

But there was perhaps much that you did not know that you learned from reading this book—especially if you had at least three different opportunities to experience this information! In this chapter, we summarise the previous chapters and bring together the significant ideas that have implications for how we teach. In doing so, we underscore the important shift these ideas ask us to make in our thinking about good teaching and in our work with students: *If you want to understand teaching, you need to understand how children learn*. We start by summarising the significant ideas about learning that Graham's work has uncovered, then lay out what these mean for classroom teaching.

What is learning?

Learning is highly individual

The extent and nature of students' learning is much more varied than we previously believed. While the underlying learning process is essentially the same for all students, differences creep in because of differences in students' background knowledge, interests, motivations, and experiences. Most previous research has looked at students as a group rather than as individuals. Graham Nuthall's research looks at learning from the perspective of individual students. When we look at learning this way, we see that most students already know about 40 to 50 percent of what the teacher is going to teach them. However—and this is the key point—this prior knowledge differs dramatically from one student to the next. Because of these individual differences in prior knowledge, as well as differences in the way students engage with classroom activities, each student experiences the classroom differently, so much so that about a third of what a student learns is unique to that student; it is not learned by other students in the class.

Why is this exactly? Well, learning involves making connections between new information and prior knowledge. If students begin an activity with different background knowledge, and they experience the activity differently, then it is not surprising they learn different things. Over time, students achieve significantly different learning outcomes even in the same classroom and from the same activities. What students learn, the experiences that help give birth to learning, and the extent of the learning are all highly individual.

Learning usually involves a progressive change in what a student knows or can do

Learning is rarely a one-shot affair. Single, isolated experiences seldom give birth to learning. What creates or shapes learning is a sequence of events or experiences, each one building on the effects of the previous one. By studying the continuous experiences of individual students, Graham Nuthall showed us that the accumulation of at least three different sets of complete information about a concept makes the difference between a concept that is never quite learned and one that firmly connects to and integrates with previous knowledge, and hence is learned and remembered.

That a certain amount of information is needed for a student to understand and learn a concept makes sense. It is as if the mind has a valve to protect it from incidental, unimportant information. Only information that connects to other related information and is encountered on a number of different occasions seems to have the critical mass necessary to get through the valve to become a part of a student's store of knowledge, skills, and beliefs. First, a student has to make sense of new experiences by relating them to already known concepts and evaluating them against that information. Next, he or she has to hold the new experiences in working memory and to connect and integrate them with related successive experiences. These processes take time and go on alongside parallel processes occurring with a multitude of other concepts. A combination of experiences is needed to produce student learning.

Learning involves extracting information from, and making sense of, experiences

Learning does not come directly from classroom activities; learning comes from the way students experience these activities. What matters is what students extract from experiences—the sense they make of them. By looking at teaching through the eyes of individual students, and carrying out detailed analyses of students' self-talk and private social talk, Graham Nuthall revealed that students engage in an ongoing process of making sense of classroom activities to construct their own interpretations of them.

Students make sense of the activities by trying to connect them to their prior knowledge and beliefs, and to other related experiences temporarily stored in working memory. They also evaluate the new experience, and what that experience implies, against their prior knowledge and beliefs. They interact with the information according to their prior knowledge and beliefs, as well as their goals and interests, and they extract the information that they think is relevant to them. "Why has the teacher given us this task?" "What do I know about this already?" "Why do I need to do this?" It is this ongoing process of students making sense of classroom activities, and managing their participation in them, that creates the links between classroom activities and learning.

Of course, sometimes students cannot make sense of their experiences. Witness the example of Austin and Mary and their attempts to understand blackness, and Sonya's struggle to make sense of her experiences with refraction in water. In these instances, the students lacked the background knowledge to make sense of the experiences. In such instances, the information students extract from an activity is unlikely to connect to their stored knowledge and so they will forget the new information.

Learning frequently comes from student self-selected or self-generated experiences

A large proportion of a student's significant learning experiences is self-selected or self-generated rather than stemming directly from the teacher. As he tracked the specific experiences that seemed to give birth to learning a concept, Graham Nuthall revealed that many of the experiences critical to students' learning are generated by, or at least chosen by, the students themselves. In the example from the Antarctica study described in Chapter 4, the students learned, on average, about half of the concepts they learned because they were able to self-select or self-generate the activities. Of these concepts, students learned about half (that is, about 25 percent) of them because of choosing from the options provided by the teacher. They learned the other half (that is, 25 percent) because of activities they themselves had created or because of talk they engaged in spontaneously with their peers. Working on a self-chosen topic for a reading or writing activity, asking questions, adding a diagram to a report, or talking with peers about relevant (or irrelevant) content all contribute to what students learn or do not learn.

Moreover, as we have seen, there is tremendous variation in the extent to which students learn from these self-selected or self-generated experiences. So much so that differences in ability are more the product of differences in the sorts of activities students choose, and in the way students manage their involvement with these activities, than the other way round.

Learning of curriculum content inextricably interweaves with the experiences and activities in which the content is encountered, and with the pervasive peer culture

This last point about learning is subtle. Students learn not just the curriculum content but also the details of the experiences that contained the content. Students learn what they do. When Graham Nuthall asked students to recall what they remembered from their classroom experiences, he found the curriculum content wrapped up in the circumstances in which they encountered the information. Thus, how students experience an activity is as much a part of what they learn as is the intended curriculum content. For example, when students sit listening to a lecture, they learn that learning happens by passively receiving information from others; when students fill out a worksheet, they learn that learning involves filling in the gaps in what someone else has created; and so on. Along with learning the curriculum content, students learn the structures and processes in which the content is embedded. It is within this framework that students "learn how to learn".

What is more, much of what students learn, and how they learn it, is bound up with their peer culture. Students live in a personal and social world as well as in the world of teacher-managed activities, and much of the knowledge that students acquire comes from their peers. When it does, it comes enveloped inside their social relationships. During class activities, what students learn and how they learn it depends on the way they interact with other students, and that interaction depends on their social status within the peer culture, as well as on the position conferred on them by the curriculum content (for example, if one student knows more about a topic than the others know). Much more than the curriculum content occupies the minds of students, and connects to what and how they learn.

Learning is multilayered

Before we outline the implications for teaching of what we now know about student learning, we pause to summarise what we know and illuminate the multilayered relationship between teaching and learning within the context of the classroom. The important idea is that how students learn from classroom activities is not simply a result of teacher-managed activities, but also the result of students' ongoing relationships with other students and of their own self-created activities or use of resources.

Figure 7.1 depicts the experiences of an individual student while learning a single concept from a sequence of activities in, say, a science class. The first three layers show, respectively, the three worlds of the classroom described in Chapter 4: the public, visible world of activities the teacher manages directly or indirectly to teach the science concept; the semiprivate, semivisible world of the student-to-student culture, relationships, and interactions; and the private, semivisible world of individual student actions. The bottom layer shows the sequence of mental processes in which the student draws on working memory as she or he acquires (or does not acquire) information about the concept.

Note that the student's learning is highly individual. Some activities help shape appropriate processes in his or her mind (shown by the circles in the bottom layer), and some do not. What is learned depends on the prior knowledge the student brings to bear to understand the information, as well as on the way the individual student participates in classroom activities. Next, note that the learning involves a progressive change in what the student knows or can do. What creates or shapes learning is a sequence of mental processes, each one building on the previous one. Note also that the links between classroom activities and mental processes are reciprocal (as are other connections between the layers). Some links are created by the teacher's design, management, and assessment of learning activities, but some are created by the student's active in-the-head attempts to understand these experiences.

In either case, what matters is the sense the student makes of the experiences and what he or she extracts from them, and this depends on his or her prior knowledge and involvement in the classroom activities. Note, again, that not all significant learning experiences come directly from the teacher-managed activities; a large

Figure 7.1: The multilayered nature of learning in the classroom

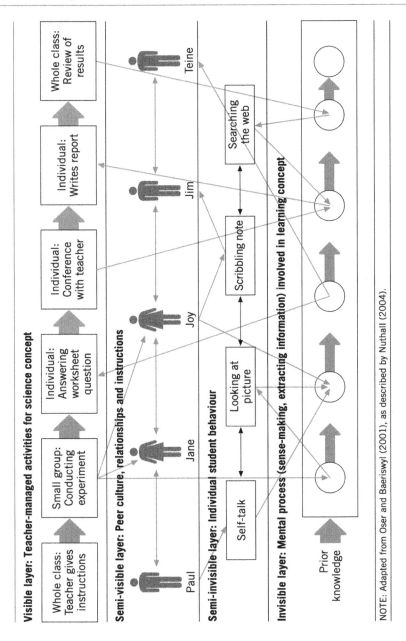

NOTE: Adapted from Oser and Baeriswyl (2001), as described by Nuthall (2004).

159

proportion come from self-selected or self-generated experiences in the private and semiprivate worlds of the student and his or her peers. These experiences might include self-talk and spontaneous peer talk.

Finally, remember that the student's memory for a concept includes not just the concept-relevant information itself. It also includes the activities and structures the student uses to learn the information—for example, the small-group experiment—as well as the student's relationships and interaction with peers.

What does this mean for teaching?

Knowing the way classroom activities affect the changes taking place in the minds of students is not all that teachers need to know, but it is at the centre of what they need to know if they are to create and adapt teaching methods and classroom management procedures in ways that help students learn. In this section, we return to the description of ideal learning activities that Graham Nuthall started with in Chapter 1, and we take what we now know about student learning and summarise the implications for teaching and teachers.

Design learning activities with students' memories in mind

Because students learn from their experiences, those of us who are teachers need to design activities in ways that students cannot avoid interacting with the information, and we need to tailor those activities to students' prior knowledge and understandings so they can make sense of them. The activities also need to be memorable. Neil Mercer, a psychologist in the United Kingdom who does work on how teachers use language to guide the learning activities of their students, puts this consideration well: "It is perhaps too often forgotten in the analysis of teaching and learning that one legitimate goal for a teacher is to make information *memorable*" (Mercer, 1995, p. 27). Graham Nuthall's work shows us that one way of making information memorable is to embed the information in a range of different activities. This practice leads to the information being experienced and stored in memory in a variety of ways, so it has a better chance of being remembered.

Because students learn what they do, we also need to choose activities that help them learn how to learn. For example, prompting students' recall of yesterday's lesson by asking questions might encourage them to use a similar self-questioning routine when they need to cue their own recall. Encouraging students to make connections between new information and prior knowledge might help them learn to make connections in other related activities. Encouraging them to evaluate the truth or consistency of a statement might help them learn to evaluate their own and other students' ideas.

Engage students in activities that enable them to revisit concepts

Because students need to experience at least three different sets of complete information about a concept before it is embedded in their network of knowledge, we need to give them opportunities to revisit concepts. As we have seen, this does not mean simple repetition. It means giving students more time on a topic and allowing them to experience the information in different ways so they can crisscross the intellectual landscape from different angles. Embedding information in different activities not only makes the information more memorable, but also enables students to revisit the concepts and ideas. When working within a set curriculum, we might decide to break a large question or problem into smaller linked questions or problems that feed into the larger question or problem. This practice gives students opportunities to revisit concepts and encourages them to make connections between experiences that involve the same concept.

Monitor individual students' evolving understanding of concepts

Because learning usually involves a progressive change in what a student knows or can do, and because it is highly individual, we need to know how our teaching practices and how the tasks we set affect what goes on in the minds of each of our students. We need to assess what each student knows and believes before the unit; and to assess what he or she knows and believes after the unit. Only then can we ascertain how that student's understandings and beliefs have changed and infer what activities contributed (or failed to contribute) to his or her current knowledge and beliefs.

For those of us dealing with a class of 20 to 30 students, these determinations require a form of individual assessment rarely seen in most content-area teaching and one that can be difficult to implement. But it is the only form of assessment that can do justice to the individual differences among students and to the dynamic change process that is learning. Learning and understanding are evolving processes. We therefore need to know what each of our students has acquired, is still in the process of acquiring, and has not yet acquired. Only by assessing what each of our students knows and understands can we decide what to do next.

Focus on "big questions"

Because learning takes time, it is better to invest teaching time and resources in a smaller number of big questions or problems in depth, rather than in covering every aspect of the curriculum at a surface level of understanding. If we do what has been already suggested—carefully design activities with students' learning in mind, enable students to revisit concepts in different ways, and monitor individual students' evolving understanding of what they are learning—then we'll find it is extremely difficult—if not impossible—to cover the entire curriculum with equal effectiveness. Instead, we need to focus on major questions or problems that provide the most pay-off for students, namely those that are significant in the discipline and in the lives and culture of the students and, as previously indicated, those that subsume smaller linked questions or problems.

Capitalise on the peer culture to foster learning

Because much of what students learn comes from their peers, we need to become involved with the peer culture and to work with it to manage our students' learning. We need to know who, among our students, is friends with whom, who has status, what roles students adopt with respect to one another, the knowledge and beliefs students share about aspects of popular cultures—music, television, clothes—and their ways of participating and working together. As Graham Nuthall indicated in Chapter 4, this is considerably easier for those of us teaching in elementary schools than it is for those of us working in high schools. If you are a high school teacher, you might need to develop an alternative culture that entails mutual respect and co-operation—a culture where everyone feels he or she has something to contribute to classroom activities, where everyone takes responsibility for learning. This is what researchers and practitioners mean when they say teachers need to develop a "learning community".

Over time, encourage students to manage their own learning activities

Finally, because much of what students learn they learn from their self-selected or self-generated experiences, and because the way they manage their participation in these activities has such a powerful shaping force on their abilities as learners, students need to learn how to learn. A dual goal for teaching, then, is to teach the curriculum content as well as effective procedures for learning the content. Over time, students internalise the procedures into productive "habits of mind" that they can apply on their own to learn new concepts.

Ian A. G. Wilkinson is Associate Professor in the School of Teaching and Learning at the Ohio State University. He met Graham Nuthall, and became fascinated with his work, when he was on faculty at The University of Auckland during the years 1992–1999.

Richard C. Anderson is Professor of Education and Psychology and Director of the Center for the Study of Reading at the University of Illinois. He has known Graham Nuthall since the 1960s and spent two months with his research group at the University of Canterbury in 1999.

References

Alton-Lee, A., Nuthall, G., & Patrick, J. (1989). Take your brown hand off my book: Racism in the classroom. *set: Research Information for Teachers, 1*, Item 8, 1–6.

Alton-Lee, A., Nuthall, G., & Patrick, J. (1993). Reframing classroom research: A lesson from the private world of children. *Harvard Educational Review, 63*(1), 50–84.

Berliner, D. C., & Biddle, B. J. (1995). *The manufactured crisis*. Reading, USA: Addison-Wesley.

Brophy, J. (2006). Graham Nuthall and social constructivist teaching: Research-based cautions and qualifications. *Teaching and Teacher Education, 22*(5), 529–537.

Cassidy, S. (2004). Learning styles: An overview of theories, models, and measures. *Educational Psychology, 24*(4), 419–444.

Clay, M. (1995). *Reading recovery: A guidebook for teachers in training*. Portsmouth, NH: Heinemann.

Clay, M. (2000). *Running records for classroom teachers*. Portsmouth, NH: Heinemann.

Collins, S. (2005). *"Excuse me, do we put a border around it?" The culture of learning that provides for opportunities for students to learn or not learn in middle school classrooms*. Unpublished doctoral thesis, University of Canterbury, Christchurch, New Zealand.

Dahl, K., & Freppon, P. (1995). A comparison of inner-city children's interpretations of reading and writing instruction in the early grades in skills-based and whole-language classrooms. *Reading Research Quarterly, 30,* 50–74.

Good, T. L., & Brophy, J. E. (2002). *Looking in classrooms.* New York: Harper and Row.

Hopkins, D., & Stern, D. (1996). Quality teachers, quality schools: International perspectives and policy implications. *Teaching and Teacher Education, 12,* 501–517.

Jackson, P. (1968). *Life in classrooms.* New York: Holt, Rinehart and Winston.

Kounin, J. (1970). *Discipline and group management in classrooms.* New York: Holt, Rinehart and Winston.

Leach, J., & Scott, P. (2002). Designing and evaluating science teaching sequences: An approach drawing upon the concept of learning demand and a social constructivist perspective on learning. *Studies in Science Education, 38,* 115–142.

Mehan, H., Okamoto, D., & Adam, J. (1996). *Constructing school success: The consequences of untracking low achieving students.* New York: Cambridge University Press.

Mercer, N. (1995). *The guided construction of knowledge: Talk amongst teachers and learners.* Clevedon, England: Multilingual Matters.

Morine-Dershimer, G. (1985). Gender, classroom organization, and grade level as factors in pupil perceptions of peer interaction. In L. C. Wilkinson & C. B. Marrett (Eds.), *Gender influences in classroom interaction* (Chapter 11). New York: Academic Press.

Mullis, I.V.A., Martin, M.O., Gonzales, E.J., Gregory, K.D., Garden, R.A., O'Connor, K.M., et al. (2000). *TIMMS 1999. International mathematics report. Findings from IEA's repeat of the Third International Mathematics and Science Study at the eighth grade.* Boston, MA: The International Study Center, Lynch School of Education, Boston College.

Nichols, S. L., & Berliner, D. C. (2005, March). *The inevitable corruption of indicators and educators through high-stakes testing.* Education Policy Studies Laboratory, #EPSL–0503–1–1–EPRU. Tempe, AZ: Arizona State University.

Nuthall, G. (1997). Understanding student thinking and learning in the classroom. In B. J. Biddle., T. L. Good, & I. F. Goodson (Eds.), *International Handbook of Teachers and Teaching,* Vol. II (pp. 681–768). Dordrecht, The Netherlands: Kluwer Academic.

Nuthall, G. (1999). Learning how to learn: The evolution of students' minds through the social processes and culture of the classroom. *International Journal of Educational Research, 31,* 139–256.

Nuthall, G. (2001). *Procedures for identifying the information content of student classroom experiences and predicting student learning.* Accessible on the Graham Nuthall website www.nuthalltrust.org.nz

Nuthall, G. (2004). Relating classroom teaching to student learning: A critical analysis of why research has failed to bridge the theory-practice gap. *Harvard Educational Review, 74*(3), 273–306.

Nuthall, G. (2005). The cultural myths and the realities of teaching and learning. In B. Webber (compiler), *The Herbison Lectures 1999–2004* (pp. 77–103). Wellington: New Zealand Council for Educational Research.

Nuthall, G., & Alton-Lee, A. (1993). Predicting learning from student experience of teaching: A theory of student knowledge construction in classrooms. *American Educational Research Journal, 30*(4), 799–840.

Organisation for Economic Co-operation and Development. (1994). *Quality in teaching.* Paris: Author.

Oser, F. K., & Baeriswyl, F. J. (2001). Choreographies of teaching: Bridging instruction to learning. In V. Richardson (Ed.), *Handbook of research on teaching* (4th ed.) (pp. 1031–1065). Washington, DC: American Educational Research Association.

O'Toole, V. (2005). *The role of emotion in children's learning task engagement in the elementary school classroom.* Unpublished doctoral thesis, University of Canterbury, Christchurch, New Zealand.

Piaget, J. (1928). *Judgment and reasoning in the child*. London: Routledge & Kegan Paul.

Pressley, M. (1994). State-of-the-science primary-grades reading instruction or whole language? *Educational Psychologist, 29,* 211–215.

Rathgen, E. (2006). In the voice of teachers: The promise and challenge of participating in classroom-based research for teachers' professional learning. *Teaching and Teacher Education, 22*(5), 580–591.

Shavelson, R. J. (2006). On the integration of formative assessment in teaching and learning: Implications for new pathways in teacher education. In F. Oser, F. Achtenhagen, & U. Renold (Eds.), *Competence-oriented teacher training: Old research demands and new pathways*. Utrecht, The Netherlands: Sense Publishers.

Stahl, S., McKenna, M., & Panucco, J. (1994). The effects of whole language instruction: An update and a reappraisal. *Educational Psychologist, 29,* 175–185.

Additional classroom-research publications by G. A. Nuthall

Nuthall, G. A. (1999). The way students learn: Acquiring knowledge from an integrated science and social studies unit. *Elementary School Journal, 99,* 303–341.

Nuthall, G. A. (2000). *How children remember what they learn in school.* Wellington: New Zealand Council for Educational Research.

Nuthall, G. A. (2000). The anatomy of memory in the classroom: Understanding how students acquire memory processes from classroom activities in science and social studies units. *American Educational Research Journal, 37,* 247–304.

Nuthall, G. A. (2000). The role of memory in the acquisition and retention of knowledge in science and social studies units. *Cognition and Instruction, 18,* 83–139.

Nuthall, G. A. (2001). Understanding how classroom experiences shape students' minds. *Unterrichtswissenschaft: Zeitschrift für Lernforschung, 29,*(3), 224–267.

Nuthall, G. A. (2002). Social constructivist teaching and the shaping of students' knowledge and thinking. In J. Brophy (Ed.), *Social constructivist teaching: Affordances and constraints* (pp. 43–79). New York: Elsevier.

Nuthall, G. A. (2005). The cultural myths and realities of classroom teaching and learning: A personal journey. *Teachers College Record, 107*(5), 895–934.

Nuthall, Graham. (2006). Bridging the gaps: the interactive effects of instruction and social processes on student experience and learning outcomes in science and social studies activities. In Fritz K. Oser, Frank Achtenhagen & Ursula Renold (Eds.) *Competence Oriented Teacher Training*, Rotterdam, The Netherlands: Sense Publishers.

Nuthall, G. A., & Alton-Lee, A. G. (1995). Assessing classroom learning: How students use their knowledge and experience to answer classroom achievement test questions in science and social studies. *American Educational Research Journal, 32*(1), 185–223.

Nuthall, G. A., & Alton-Lee, A. G. (1997). *Understanding learning in the classroom.* Report to the Ministry of Education. Understanding Learning and Teaching Project 3. Wellington: Ministry of Education.

Other related publications

Bourke, C. (Producer). (2004, 21 February). Interview with Graham Nuthall. *Saturday Morning with Kim Hill* [Radio broadcast]. Wellington: Radio New Zealand.

Kaur, B. (Ed.) (2006). Graham Nuthall's legacy: Understanding teaching and learning [Special issue]. *Teaching and Teacher Education, 22*(5), 525–626.

For further information

www.nuthalltrust.org.nz

The Graham Nuthall Classroom Research Trust
School of Education
University of Canterbury
PO Box 4800
Christchurch
New Zealand

Index

examples of concepts and ideas 113
experiences, learning from a variety of
    107–27, 155–6, 161
explicit concept definition 108, 124, 125,
    126

Freud, Sigmund 74

grade scores 30
graduation qualifications 40

ideas and perceptions, reconciling 109–10,
    116–23, 161
implicit concept definition 108, 124, 125,
    126
individual variations in learning 26, 86,
    100–4, 154–5, 158, 161–2
information
    access to 92–3, 94, 101
    additional and background 124, 125,
    126
    different kinds experienced by students
    108–14
    embedding in range of different
    activities 160, 161
    implicit or partial 124, 125, 126
    making memorable 160
    preparatory or contextual 124, 125, 126
intelligence, see ability
interaction of teachers and students 23–7
internalisation 37, 74, 150, 163
International Association for the
    Evaluation of Educational Achievement
    40–1
Internet 51
item files 62, 68, 84–7

knowledge 43–4, 50, 104. See also
    learning; memory; understanding
knowledge, prior 124, 125, 126, 158, 159
    and ability 98, 129
    and posttest scores 98

connection of new experiences with
    71–2, 73, 58, 158, 160, 161
    impact on understanding 80, 104
    individual differences in 100, 101,
    154–5
    lack of 77–8, 114–23, 156
    number of students who have 34
    percentage of items already known,
    Antarctic unit 99
    story of Rata 132, 139
    testing and interviewing students for
    information about 58, 59, 62, 129–30
    See also learning; understanding

language 74, 75, 160
learning
    and change in beliefs and
    understandings 34, 51–2, 155, 159, 160,
    161–4
    and classroom behaviour 35
    and motivation 33–4, 40–1
    and spontaneous peer talk 83, 84,
    85–93, 102, 160
    beliefs about 21–2
    how students learn 69–73, 163
    how students learn from variety of
    experiences 107–27, 155–6, 161
    individual variations in 26, 86, 100–4,
    154–5, 158, 161–2
    multilayered nature of 158–60
    prediction of 63, 124–7
    role of ability in 97–103
    students learn what they do 35, 157
    Year 7 example of 64–9
    See also ethnic differences in learning;
    knowledge; memory; understanding
learning activities 104, 125, 126, 158
    characteristics of 36–7
    designing 36, 160–1
    enabling students to revisit concepts
    161
    evaluating 51–2

Lightning Source UK Ltd.
Milton Keynes UK
UKOW05f2106170116

266488UK00006B/118/P